LILLIAN TOO'S
198 Feng Shui Ways to
Transform Your Life

LILLIAN TOO'S
198 Feng Shui Ways to
Transform Your Life

CICO BOOKS
LONDON NEW YORK

Published in 2011 by CICO Books
an imprint of Ryland Peters & Small
20–21 Jockey's Fields, London WC1R 4BW
519 Broadway, 5th, Floor, New York NY 10012

www.cicobooks.co.uk

10 9 8 7 6 5 4 3 2 1

A CIP catalogue record for this book is available from the
British Library

ISBN-11: 978 1 907563 31 7

Printed in China

Editor: Robin Gurdon
Designer: Fahema Khanam
Illustrators: Stephen Dew and Anthony Duke

Contents

CHAPTER THREE
Transforming Your Thought Energy

CHAPTER FOUR
Special Techniques For Success

Introduction

It gives me so much joy to bring this beautiful new book to all my readers as we enter a time where I am feeling so energized and excited at introducing the *third dimension of spiritual feng shui* to the world! If you have been yearning for a change, a kick-start to better and new things, or just to infuse new energy into your life, then this is the book that is just perfect for you. It is a hand-book containing all of my most favorite feng shui tips, those which I have personally used in my own life, and for the lives of my children and my closest friends; tips that have worked wonders for me and for them.

When you follow the advice compiled into this lovely book you will see how easy it is to implement simple little changes, such as rearranging your furniture or re-orientating your

facing direction, that can turn out to have a real impact in triggering life-altering changes that seem to work like magic. Feng shui is effective and works very quickly. In many cases you will experience almost immediate results. For example, I know a woman who had difficulty in getting recognized at work. She read my column and in it I advised that those who wish to be recognized at work can install a bright light in the South of their homes and keep it turned on. Within a week of doing this, this lady was asked to present a piece of work in front of a group of very senior directors of her company. She impressed all of them and soon got promoted to handling high-profile projects for the company!

Anyone can do it!

So you see, it really is that simple! Transforming your life is definitely within your ability, *anyone's* ability—especially when you know how to use *all three dimensions of feng shui to make the energy in your environment work for you*. Looking at the last 20 years of my life, I have observed how my own life and the lives of all my students have steadily changed for the better; and they have done this simply by making adjustments to their living space through clever use of feng shui, and tweaking the energy of their homes according to the cyclic changes of time with the use of auspicious symbols and strategically placed elements. Just using these two dimensions of *space* and *time* feng shui, they have seen prosperity and fortune enter their lives, and happiness creeps in wondrous ways that they have never imagined possible!

My own experience

Something happened to me about 13 years ago which I didn't forsee coming. I tell this story because when I look back, it has become clear to me that all things happen for a reason. My good feng shui has led me to discovering something very special and it is not a coincidence that you have picked up this special book and are now reading this little introduction that my publishers

asked me to write! Anyway, about 13 years ago, I was walking past my fax machine, which was buzzing away, and something made me look to see who the fax was from. It turned out that I had a fan who was a *Lama*. I felt very honoured so I wrote back to say thanks! And a month later I received such precious presents from this mysterious Lama and an invitation to visit him in India!

Spiritual feng shui

That year, my friends, I met my personal spiritual Guru, the most precious Kyajbe Lama Zopa Rinpoche. It was such a wonderful and blissful experience and I have followed my special Guru for 13 years now. In his infinite kindness and generosity, he showed me that there was a third and vital dimension of feng shui practice that worked beautifully alongside the two dimensions of feng shui I already knew so well. This is the *spiritual dimension of feng shui*, one that involves generating the good heart and the motivation to benefit others; in the process, gaining access and communication with the cosmic forces that empower one's feng shui so strongly. It became clear to me that the practice of feng shui in the

space and time dimension, while very effective, was *incomplete*! I realized that all the greatest feng shui masters I had ever had the honour and privilege to meet were *expert meditators* who were skilled in the *art of manipulating energy at a cosmic level*, at a *spiritual* level.

So my dear friends, it makes me so thrilled to be able to share some of what I have learnt with you in this book. I have included chapters on how you can begin to tap the cosmic dimension by using meditation and visualization. I've talked about space cleansing and how you can use incense offerings to alter the energy in your space at a cosmic level. Please do enjoy this book and use it as your personal stepping stone to a new life, filled with happiness, prosperity, and good health! If something has worked well for you, please do write in as it really makes my day to hear from you my readers! And if you need more information about feng shui go visit our website at www.wofs.com, where there are amazing goodies all for you FREE!

Looking forward to meeting you soon
Lillian Too

Chapter One

Transforming Your Living Space

Activating the energy of the space in which we live can make a huge difference to our well-being. The key to our vigour and our strength, our success and our happiness lies in the quality of the energy within us and in our surroundings. The best place to begin to learn about revitalizing energy is our most familiar territory—the home.

Having plentiful, positive chi in the home is vital—energy levels are affected by the combination of yin and yang, the inclusion of positive elements, and the beneficial use of colour. If you can follow the simple rules governing their use, you will be well on the way to receiving their positive benefits.

Always remember that chi energy is around us and our homes, so it is essential to learn to harness it, making it work for you. None of the following tips is complicated but each will successfully enhance your home while giving you a solid basis on which to build the rest of your feng shui knowledge.

Tuning into the life force–the chi

1

Everyone can develop greater sensitivity to energy, the divinely charged spirit that gives life to us and to our homes. It is an intangible life force that molds our emotions, defines our moods, sustains our strength, and feeds our being. At birth, this spirit is pure and fresh, but as one grows into maturity and old age, it becomes colored by our experiences of life. Some of these colors expand our horizons; others make us wilt.

When we move into a brand-new home with its clean, pure energy, the smell of paint still lingering in its rooms, the spirit of the home seems vital and vibrant. When a home's life force is lively and dominated by vibrant yang energy, its inhabitants' moods tend to be positive and happy.

Over time, the energy of the home grows stale and tired. Exhaustion creeps in when yin chi accumulates, overwhelming the vitality of yang chi. Unless the energy of the home is revitalized, the chi becomes stale, bringing weakness and lethargy to its inhabitants. Their vitality suffers; good luck gets caught in a negative spiral so that, at best, boredom becomes the order of the day and, at worst, serious misfortunes, illnesses, and accidents occur. Happiness becomes an increasingly rare thing in such households.

A Kirlian image of hands that expresses the body's auric energy as an imprint.

What causes tired energy?

Mainly it is clutter—physical, emotional, and spiritual clutter—that engulfs spaces and faces. It preys on us like an invisible monster, silently creeping into our homes and draining the energy there, When we finally become aware of its presence, our energies are already so sapped that we often lack the motivation to get rid of it.

The most debilitating effect of clutter is the way it convolutes energy within space. Although not all clutter that builds up is bad, much of it is.

Everyone needs to do chi maintenance—of the home, mind, and body. We need to clean out the stale energy created by the junk that builds up in our homes, mental attitudes, and hearts. This dejunking process will revitalize us as nothing else can. When you do this, you brush away bad energy, shrugging off outdated attitudes and making space for new energy to enter.

Every living thing is thought to emit a life force, or chi. This can be captured by aura photography, which reveals intrinsic energy as color.

2 Assessing yin and yang chi

Have you ever entered someone's home and felt that the atmosphere is unbalanced, not in sync, or just seriously disturbed? If you are sensitive to energy, you might also feel sick, or as if you are choking, or in need of air. Sometimes strange energy manifests in the onslaught of a massive headache. These are indications that the chi of the house or building you are visiting may be in conflict with your chi, or that perhaps the energy there is so yin that it disturbs your balance.

Yang chi sustains us. When we encounter spaces that are too yin, we react. These reactions manifest more keenly in those who have acute sensitivity to energy or in those who are accustomed to working with it.

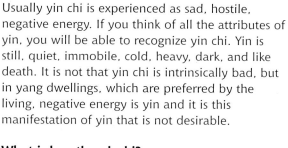

Usually yin chi is experienced as sad, hostile, negative energy. If you think of all the attributes of yin, you will be able to recognize yin chi. Yin is still, quiet, immobile, cold, heavy, dark, and like death. It is not that yin chi is intrinsically bad, but in yang dwellings, which are preferred by the living, negative energy is yin and it is this manifestation of yin that is not desirable.

What is heartbreak chi?

When we focus our attention on the chi of any home, we can pick up the vibrations that dominate the house. If its occupants are sad, you will pick up a sense of pervasive melancholia. Sometimes the air can be so thick with despondency that you become imbued with despondency too. Sad homes contain illness and heartbreak chi that tends to sap the yang spirit. This is because the home is hungry for yang chi. Such homes create depression, hopelessness, and a resigned air.

It is also possible to sense killing chi, if it is present. This kind of hostility emanates from walls and ceilings. If you are sensitive to chi, you will feel the presence of invisible knives and arrows that create uncomfortable sensations. This kind of chi is very harmful and can be dangerous, causing illness, loss, and accidents to befall residents.

Houses with negative chi energy do sap their inhabitants' spiritual vitality. Such places are characterized by a strong feeling of lethargy. Homes like these really need to be revitalized and given a shot of living-movement chi.

Pay attention to yin rooms such as the bedroom and bathroom. These are quiet spaces, but they still need vitality.

Physical afflictions create bad spatial feng shui   3

Modern homes are designed with so many corners, pillars, levels, and shapes that, quite unknowingly, they could be creating secret "poison arrows". To become aware of the number of sharp, straight, and pointed features inside and outside your home, and the energy they create, all you need do is look around you. Unless your attention is drawn to these physically jarring features and their killing vibrations, it is surprisingly easy to miss them. But as soon as you become aware of the dynamics and influences they exert on your immediate physical environment, you will have taken the first step toward that ancient, yet still relevant, practice of feng shui.

What to look out for

Be aware of anything straight and long, such as a straight road aimed right at your front door (see also Tip 5), or a long internal corridor "hitting" the door to the master bedroom. Also, note anything sharp, such as the edge of a nearby building directed at

Look out for feng shui afflictions around your home – such as pylons, trees, and the edges of nearby buildings that appear to "hit" your home.

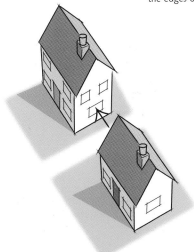

Rooflines of buildings in close proximity to your home can create external "poison arrows", or shar chi – negative energy that afflicts your living space. It is vital to check for environmental feng shui problems before you begin to address the feng shui within your home's interior.

your house, or the edge of a pillar in the living room hitting the place you regularly sit. Equally, beware anything triangular in shape, such as the roof line of a neighbor's house aimed at your front door or one of your windows (see left), or an abstract painting hanging above your living-room fireplace that features sharp, triangular shapes. All of these environmental afflictions can create slivers of arrows hitting you, so now it's time to stop living with them—and take action. Read on to discover the feng shui remedies you'll need.

4   Neutralize hurtful buildings

Although most of us are stuck in our present location and it is usually quite hard to counter bad energy in the external environment, it is better, nevertheless, to be aware of anything that may be creating problems for your home in terms of surrounding energy. Once you develop your powers of observation, turn your attention to the environment around you, looking for both natural and man-made features outside.

What hurt most are tall and hostile-looking buildings that directly face your house. Large structures that stand right in front of your house usually cause obstacles in your life, creating blocking energies that bring misfortune and cause you to fail.

Which destructive energy could affect your home?

• A home that sits **south** (facing north) is a fire-element house, so if the building opposite you is a curvilinear shape and is predominantly blue or black, signifying water, the energy being sent your way represents killing energy. It must be neutralized with earth element energy. Solve this problem by building a brick wall in front of your house.

• If your home sits **north** (facing south) it is said to be a water-element house. If the building opposite is round and predominantly yellow, signifying earth, the energy being sent your way represents destructive energy—it must be neutralized with wood-element energy. Planting a tree or growing a hedge will combat this.

Size and shape matter

Some buildings are more harmful than others. Those with many corners and edges are the source of the greatest amounts of negative energy. When buildings are tilted, thereby causing their edges to point directly at your home, it is very dangerous. The edge of a building is like a knife-edge that sends very sharp killing energy your way.

The color of tiles and walls of buildings, as well as the shape of the building itself, can be a severe problem especially if the colors and shapes represent elements unfriendly to the element of your home.

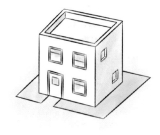

• A home that sits **east** (facing west) or southeast (ie facing northwest) is a wood-element house, so if the building opposite is square and predominantly white or metallic, thereby signifying metal, the energy being sent your way represents destructive energy, which must be neutralized with fire-element energy—try installing bright lights.

• When your home sits **west** (facing east) or **northwest** (facing southeast), it is a metal-element house. A triangular-shaped building that is predominantly red, signifying fire, will send destructive energy your way—neutralize it with water-element energy by building a small fountain.

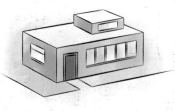

• If your home sits **northeast** (facing southwest) or **south-west** (facing northeast), it is an earth-element house, and if the building opposite is rectangular and mostly brown or green, signifying wood, the energy coming your way represents destructive energy. Neutralize it with metal-element energy; using a windchime will help.

Beware the straight road at a T-junction

5

The number of roads that directly face your house can have a serious impact on its feng shui. Generally speaking, the T-junction is one of the deadliest since this means the house or building directly faces a long, straight road. When the traffic is moving fast towards the house or building the feng shui is extraordinarily bad as it hits the building with killing energy, called shar chi; and when the traffic is flowing away from the building it is taking away all the wealth of the building with it. So either way a straight road in front of your house, or even in front of your apartment building, brings bad luck. Thus the T-junction is super bad news whichever way the road moves.

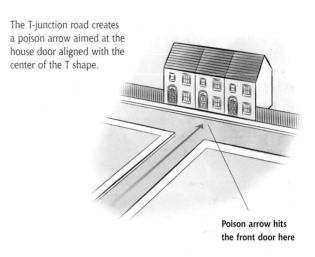

The T-junction road creates a poison arrow aimed at the house door aligned with the center of the T shape.

Poison arrow hits the front door here

Poison arrows

Poison arrows are an example of seriously afflicted energy in your external environment. Remember, anything straight that is aimed directly at your

T-junction properties can be less afflicted by poison arrows if they are raised above the level of the road.

house, and especially your front door, is like having killing energy 'shooting' the residents.

When there are two buildings with a narrow road separating them directly in front of your house, the effect is considered severe. The road's energy is similar to that of the straight road possessing the energy of a harmful poison arrow aimed at your house. This effect can cause accidents and misfortune.

People living in houses hit by such unfriendly energy are sure to experience difficulties manifesting in different areas of their life, and many of these difficulties cause distress and have tragic consequences. The Chinese have always avoided straight roads pointed directly at their homes or their offices. If your home is elevated above the level of the road however the T-junction road is not so harmful, otherwise it is considered a cardinal source of negative energy.

6 The effect of feeder roads

When you look at the roads that flow past your home, first note if the road is beneficial or harmful. The effect is said to be beneficial when traffic on the road is moving slowly and in a gentle curve toward your home. This effect is increased if there are feeder roads joining the road before it moves past your main entrance as it is bringing more than one source of wealth to your building. Feeder roads are thus good news in this context. However, if the road passing your home is fast-moving and harmful then the feeder roads are said to be adding negative energy to the road, and the harmful effect is then increased.

Movement of
chi energy

Feeder roads, such as small sliproads with little traffic, are not harmful to the feng shui of your home.

7 Becoming aware of harmful man-made structures

Structures such as transmission towers, large factory chimneys, or telecommunication towers are infamous for the massive doses of shar chi they send out, and this "killing breath" is often hard to combat. They may cause illness to those living in houses or apartments nearby. Electricity transmission towers may be especially harmful, and it is advisable to avoid living too close to these buildings.

Other potentially harmful structures that can cause feng shui problems for you if you live too near them are big steel and chrome bridges, power stations, and other massive concrete and steel edifices.

Be extremely wary of man-made constructions. They are not only threatening; they are also often the source of killing energy, especially when they face your home directly. Put some visual distance between you and such structures by planting some trees to create a barrier of leaves between them and your home.

Triangular-shaped roofs can create poison arrows

Bamboo screening can help shield some negativity from neighbors' buildings

Take a look over the terrace or balcony—you may have high walls or fencing around you, but external structures can still influence the feng shui of your property.

Determine the killing element correctly

8

Here's how to diagnose the element of killing energy so that you can counter its effects with a cure. There are only five elements, but choosing the right one is crucial for the cure to work. You need to be familiar with the killing cycle of the elements:

• Wood kills earth
• Earth kills water
• Water kills fire
• Fire kills metal
• Metal kills wood

Use a compass to determine the source direction of killing energy that is directly hitting your home, and especially your main front door. Every direction is associated with an element. Once you have established the element of killing energy, you can determine the element that will deflect its harmful effects and act as a cure.

The deflecting element cycle

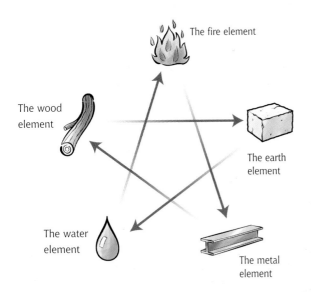

The fire element

The wood element

The earth element

The water element

The metal element

ENERGY TIP

Check your directions

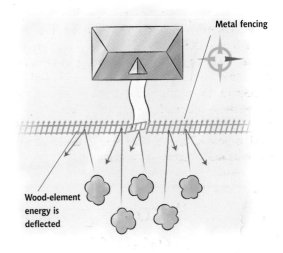

Metal fencing

Wood-element energy is deflected

Metal energy deflects negative wood energy hitting the home.

The elements associated with directions are as follows:

South	Fire	Water
North	Water	Earth
East & southeast	Wood	Metal
West & northwest	Metal	Fire
Southwest & northeast	Earth	Wood

Use the chart above to discover which element is potentially harmful and its relevant cure. Some examples are:

• When the source of killing energy is south, use a fountain of water to deflect fire
• When the source of killing energy is north, use a concrete wall to signify earth to soak away water
• When the source of killing energy is east or southeast, use metal railings to enclose the wood
• When the source of killing energy is west or northwest, use bright lights to melt away metal
• When the source of killing energy is southwest or northeast, use a hedge to signify wood to cover the earth

9   Use protective elements creatively

Take note of your home's elements and shapes: the rectangular shape of the window shutters is associated with wood.

You can be as creative as you like in thinking up cures to suppress or counter harmful energy as both a specific color and shape, as well as its intrinsic nature, can represent each of the five elements.

For example, the **fire** element can be symbolized by the triangular shape and the color red, as well as by candles, bright lights, chandeliers, spotlights, the sun, and by anything hot. Fire is also signified by upward movement and it cannot really be stored, it needs to be created afresh. Fire in feng shui signifies yang energy.

The **wood** element is usually associated with plants, wooden furniture, the colors green and brown, the rectangular shape, and any kind of growing vegetation. Wood is the only element that can "grow" and its movement is upwards and sideways. Wood in feng shui signifies growth.

The **water** element is symbolized by anything liquid and the colors blue and black. Water is fluid, with a downward movement. The shape of water is generally

accepted to be wavy. Water in feng shui signifies wealth and income. The **earth** element can be represented by rocks, stones, concrete, walls, crystals, or anything that is square in shape. Pictures of mountains and planets also signify earth, as well as the colors beige and yellow. Earth is also synonymous with relationship and health luck.

The **metal** element is signified by anything made of metal such as gold, silver, brass, or steel. The round shape is also symbolic of metal. In feng shui, metal energy signifies the energy of the unbending leader or head of the family. Metal is the most unyielding of the elements and can be used as a very effective cure to combat many feng shui ills.

Both this red door (right) and the triangular shapes created by this line of rooftops (below), denote a profusion of fire-element energy.

Afflictions are caused by intangible bad chi 10

Knowing about physical feng shui really is only half the picture. To be truly effective you need to go beyond repairing the physical problems of feng shui within your home. This brings us to the realm of the changing energy patterns that affect us, and these are caused by intangible forces. These forces are explained in the different formulas of feng shui, which enable us to draw up luck maps and feng shui charts of houses.

These charts reveal secrets that point the way for us to make good luck better and bad luck bearable. The secrets of the feng shui charts have, in recent years, amazed a growing number of people through their sheer effectiveness. Many are discovering that just about anyone can learn to understand feng shui charts and use the relevant ones to improve their prospects and enjoy a happier lifestyle.

In feng shui, energy moves around the world in 20-year cycles, or periods.

together to create patterns and concentrations of good and bad luck. So afflictions—illness, loss of income, accidents, job obstacles, and all other types of misfortune—can manifest into physical space caused by nothing more than the passage of time. When you know how to identify these cyclical causes of bad luck and learn how to overcome their pernicious effects, you will be maximizing your use of feng shui.

A change to the time period also influences the collective unconscious of the world's peoples. So in the preceding period of 7 the pursuit of wealth was a priority, whereas in the current period of 8 you will find that people become more introspective, pursuing relationships and health issues more keenly.

As time passes, the world's chi energy changes, which impacts upon the luck of your home.

Cyclical movements of energy

Different feng shui charts reveal the way energy is distributed in the various sectors of the home from one period to the next. This energy is the invisible chi that brings both good luck and misfortune, and it does so in a cyclical way. This invisible chi energy is constantly transforming from good to bad and to good again over periods of time—periods of time that are expressed as months, as years, and as 20-year periods. Think of them as cyclical movements of energy that are continuously and simultaneously rotating. Thus, in any moment of time, different daily, monthly, yearly, and period cyclical energies are coming

11 The Lo Pan compass identifies intangible energy

Take the time to study ways in which to detect good and bad intangible energy in your living space. This is a skill worth acquiring and involves using a compass—the methods used to map out the luck sectors of homes are expressed as compass directions, so it really is impossible to go very deeply into the subject without using the compass to obtain your bearings. There is a special need for accuracy here, as feng shui does not stop at dividing orientations into just eight directions. On the Lo Pan compass used by feng shui practitioners, each direction is divided into three sub-directions, giving a total of 24.

Q & A

Q: What are the 24 mountains of the compass?

A: The 24 mountains is the collective name for the 24 sub-directions of the compass. Feng shui flying star charts are drawn up on the basis of these 24 directions, or "mountains", each of which take up 15 degrees of compass space. The chi energy is different for each one, depending upon the age and facing direction of the house.

The Lo Pan compass

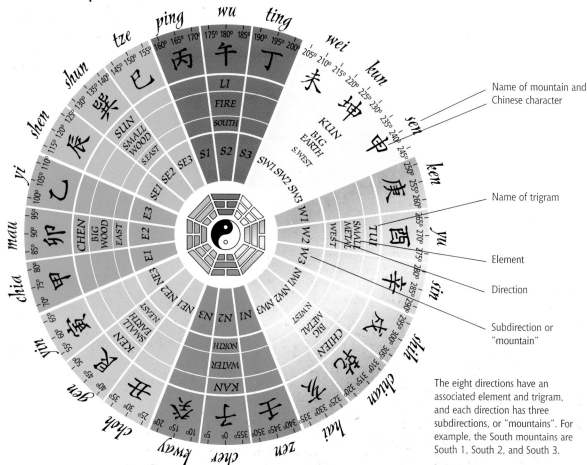

Name of mountain and Chinese character

Name of trigram

Element

Direction

Subdirection or "mountain"

The eight directions have an associated element and trigram, and each direction has three subdirections, or "mountains". For example, the South mountains are South 1, South 2, and South 3.

Counter negative energy with new chi

12

Negative energy is best countered by bringing new energy into a living space. New energy is young, fresh, and has great vitality; it replenishes any home, keeping the chi that is inside it robust and growing.

Bringing in new chi

Chinese Taoist masters always stress that the relationship of yin and yang must be assessed according to their strength and vigor. It is important to sense whether yang energy is young or old so that one can differentiate between strong yang or dissipating yang. Yang energy that has grown old is exhausted and will turn into yin unless it is reinvigorated and given new energy.

Move your furniture around

To keep the chi moving I do this at least once a year two weeks before the lunar New Year (in early February); you can do this before western New Year or during the Christmas holidays. It is amazing how much strength I feel flowing into my body each January when I start this major house re-energizing exercise. As well as cleaning in every corner of your home, include the rituals and cleansing ceremonials that appeal to you, for they generate positive shifts of the intangible forces that enhance the energy of your home.

Remodel your home

Redecorate every three to four years. It can be enough to just clean and repaint the walls; at other times more serious renovations, in accordance with changing Flying Stars, may be undertaken. This can involve placing a water feature in a certain corner, changing a door into a window, or expanding a room because favorable chi is flying into it. Houses always feel so good after a well-planned feng shui renovation. It causes a rush of new chi into the home, which has the most revitalizing yang effect.

Light and color bathe a home in fresh new energy. Paying attention to windows also brings in yang energy that creates vitality in your living space.

13 Stifled, locked-in energy

Negative energy can be stifled when it is trapped inside homes and offices. These are buildings whose windows and doors are seldom opened to let the air in.

In the tropics, where temperatures are so high that people live in air-conditioned homes and rooms, travel in air-conditioned cars, and work in air-conditioned offices, some people never breathe fresh air. Over time, those who have no regular regime of exercise grow sick from breathing stagnant air day after day. People in this condition are badly in need of new chi.

Breathing yang chi is a luxury for city people

In temperate countries, it is the intense cold of the winter months that causes homes to stay locked up tight, but the result is the same. The chi within these homes is recycled and so such places cry out for new energy. This is a problem that afflicts city folk, as a result of which an entire range of new ills and diseases have been discovered in the past fifty years... all caused by people living in excessively yin spaces.

Tune in to the chi of your living or working space. Consider whether there has been too much recycling of stale air in it. Try opening the doors and windows and feel the energy shift instantly. The simple act of opening doors and windows in the home, to suck in air and wind from the great outdoors, has a fabulous revitalizing effect upon it. Make the effort to revitalize enclosed spaces like this at least once a month, if not more often. You

The high windows bring in yang energy, but this is stifled by the yin of the deep-pile rug which, when the windows are closed, creates a claustrophobic environment.

will find that you need to have at least two openings (doors or windows) to create a flow of chi in an area. Simply keeping one door open will not bring in chi from the outdoors. You must facilitate this flow of energy, and then you will feel the gentle wind and breezes breathing new life into your living space.

Do this during the morning hours before your environment becomes polluted.

Spotting energy-stealers around you

14

It is easy to miss the things that bring you harm in your environment unless you concentrate on consciously registering everything that has a place in your space.

This is why you need to engage your mind one hundred percent and why it is necessary to develop a keen awareness when you look around your room, otherwise you can miss things that you would normally take for granted. Those new to feng shui almost always have preconceived ideas about what is, or is not, important from a feng shui perspective. The truth of the matter, of course, is that everything can be important. That is why it is helpful to develop an awareness of energy. This is the key to determining its impact on your feng shui.

The overhead beam creates poison arrows

Seating placed directly below the beam is afflicted

Shoes lined up by the door can create negative, blocked energy, stopping good fortune entering the home.

Watch out for the little things

An awareness of energy leads to direct communication with the spirit of a room. This helps to draw your attention to features that have a negative effect upon you; for instance, piles of newspapers in a corner corresponding to your success direction create obstacles to your success. In the hall, shoes caked with mud left near your front door will cause negative energy to be sent to the door, while a dirty ashtray in the middle of the living room or wall paint that is peeling in the northwest corner will affect the man of the family. A chip on a coffee cup usually brings hiccups to

well-laid plans; the sharp edge of a sideboard hitting you as you sleep will affect your chances of success at work, and the heavy energy of a beam directly above your bed can be the cause of migraines and tension (see Tip 18). These are things that can easily escape a busy person's attention.

If you come home tired from work each day you may not have the time or inclination to notice your surroundings, let alone become aware of things that could be hurting you, so do not be surprised if you are totally oblivious to the way energy is moving (or not moving) in your rooms. By the time you wake up to the fact that a host of energy-stealers have been pressing down on your energy, you might well be too weak to do anything—so now is the time to turn energy-detective.

15   Developing the all-seeing feng shui eye

The more clued in you are to your living space, the more observant you will become in terms of identifying the source of good and bad energy. You need to practice developing an all-seeing feng shui eye.

Zone in!

Observe the shape of the room, its height, size, and, most importantly, the orientation of sitting and/or sleeping directions based on the arrangement of the furniture. Take note of each item's shape, color, size, and placement, then see how they interact. Observe also the decorative objects, computers, and other things placed on tables, in cupboards, and in the corners. These things make up the sum total of the energy of any room. So look at everything that adds to the ambience.

Whatever the decorative style of your rooms, don't let familiar possessions become invisible. Every item impacts upon the feng shui of the room, and therefore its intrinsic energy.

Check out the art on your wall—is it positive and uplifting?

Small items such as vases still affect your feng shui

Make sure you sit facing your auspicious direction (see Tip 87)

Note here the shelf is creating a poison arrow hitting the person sat at the computer

The all-seeing feng shui eye is like a camera in your mind. Click a picture making sure that you are using a wide-angle lens, then focus on it until you remember it easily. This is a crucial part of the inner feng shui method that requires you to use your mental concentration. With a detailed and clear mental image, your efforts at creating new energy or strengthening existing energy will be much more effective.

Awareness levels always improve with practice—soon you will be able to bring an image to mind at a click of your fingers!

Use your feng shui eye to absorb every item in a room and recall the image at will.

The energy of your physical space 16

In many instances, disharmony is due to afflictions in surrounding space. These can be due to any number of physical and intangible afflictions—wrong feng shui, harmful orientations, poison arrows, killing energy, or simply stale, tired energy that has become too yin.

This last category can be the most harmful of all. It may be caused by nothing more than a daily buildup of stale, tired energy. When homes are not properly maintained, over time the energy held within them deteriorates.

Yin chi is created by dead insects, peeling paint, damp newspapers and magazines, dying plants, and junk built up over time. When stuff has been piled in corners, hidden in closets, swept under carpets, and pushed behind curtains, while objects have not been moved for a long time, the stillness

itself causes yin chi to build up. And when homes become dirty, over time grime also builds up. This kind of energy decline can be dangerous.

Gifts retained for sentimental reasons and unwanted objects left lying around create negative energy pockets all over the home which can overtake good energy sources. The energy of a home's physical space then becomes afflicted so that it has to be cleared, cleansed, and purified.

Chi and physical health

The good news is that dejunking your home is easy and revitalizing, making you feel well in the process. Clearing clutter and energizing your living and working spaces is both therapeutic and beneficial. I have found this makes such a difference to my family's sense of well-being that I have become addicted to it. My daughter says I am a compulsive dejunker. While others do spring cleaning once a year, I do it regularly, all the time.

This is because I live in a house that has grown progressively larger over the years. Space for my husband's, my daughter's, and my own rubbish to accumulate has also grown, and, unless I constantly counter our tendency to accumulate junk, the energy of my home is certain to become blocked. However, house-clearing and rearranging my furniture and decorative objects is never a chore for me. I love keeping the chi of my house flowing smoothly—it creates a feel-good ambience in the home that I have become addicted to.

Homes need constant reorganization and effective storage to avoid the buildup of clutter and promote a balanced, harmonious environment.

17 Energy-stealers in your personal space

Internal environments also have many of the energy-stealers that are commonplace in the external environment. Things that bring bad feng shui inside the home are not necessarily bad in themselves—it is usually the way they are placed and how they react to the space that causes the problem.

Thus it is necessary to be aware of the sharp edges of corners, tables, cupboards, and so forth if these edges happen to be directly pointed at the place you normally sit or sleep. In the same way overhanging hard structures such as exposed structural beams and ornate ceiling designs can send harmful energy if you happen to be sitting or sleeping, working or relaxing directly under them.

Check out what's familiar

All homes have these sources of potentially harmful energy and it is beneficial to look closely at your living and work spaces to spot exactly where

This space looks modern and comfortable, but even clutter-free spaces such as this can have hidden pitfalls that interfere with the otherwise good energy of your room.

The television has harsh, protruding glass edges. There is little softness to any of the furnishings or items in this space. This causes discomfort and can create a feeling of stress for the occupants.

Coffee table edge points directly at the seated person, sending out a poison arrow.

they may be causing problems for you. Give your space your full attention so that you analyse it with knowledgeable awareness. It is easy to miss noticing what can cause you harm inside your home or office. But once you know what to look for you can easily identify the structures, furniture, and physical objects that could be sending harming energy outwards. These are the "energy destroyers" of the living environment and they must be disarmed and made harmless. Otherwise they create the cause for illness to manifest.

Overhead beams weigh down on you

18

One of the most harmful of structures in most homes is the exposed overhead beam. Many apartments in older buildings have these harmful beams that send down killing energy to those sitting directly under them. It is worse when the apartment is on the lower floors of a high-rise building, as these structural beams are usually repeated on every floor.

Blocking bad energy

In bungalows and houses these beams are not as powerful and so are less harmful. To block the bad energy so they do not hurt any member of the household all you have to do is block these beams from views with a carefully designed ceiling... it is also good to arrange your furniture so that your favourite chair is not placed directly under these beams. In homes that have many exposed rafters and raw pieces of wood that appear part of the overall design or look of the home, the exposed beams or wood do not create harmful energy. It is only when the overhead beam sticks out like a sore thumb that they can be potentially harmful.

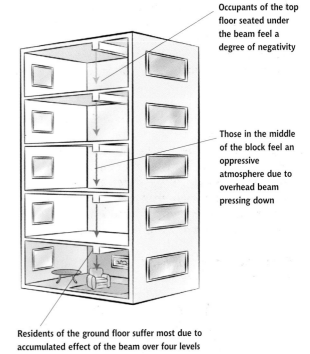

Occupants of the top floor seated under the beam feel a degree of negativity

Those in the middle of the block feel an oppressive atmosphere due to overhead beam pressing down

Residents of the ground floor suffer most due to accumulated effect of the beam over four levels

ENERGY TIP

Using bright lighting

In feng shui, lighting is an excellent cure for oppressive structures overhead.

Uplighters can help remedy the negative chi created by overhead beams in your home or office.

An excellent cure is to install lighting that is directed upwards towards the ceiling, as this has the effect of pushing the energy upwards. It also creates a very soft, subdued effect, softening the energy of a room considerably.

When in doubt, always move your seat if it is situated directly under a beam. Even when you are just visiting a friend, it is a good idea to avoid taking the seat directly under an overhead beam.

19 Keeping energy flowing smoothly for vitality

Energy that is imbued with life and vitality flows smoothly through our rooms and corridors—it is gentle, undulating, and relaxed. This kind of energy, which is completely free of tension and aggravation, is exactly the kind of energy we strive to create in every part of our homes.

In order to encourage this, feng shui practitioners ensure that furniture, plants, and other objects are arranged around the home in a manner that enables energy to flow. The way that room layouts are planned and furniture is arranged is either conducive to the flow of energy or blocks its pathways. Energy must not remain stagnant and blockages are the main reason for energy to lose its positive attributes. Remember, though, that while energy that does not move becomes sick, energy that moves too fast also turns out to be hostile and destructive. Energy that flows smoothly and naturally, moving neither too fast, nor too slowly, is good energy; it is friendly, conducive to good health, and brings good fortune.

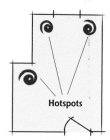

Identity the social hotspots in a room, where people tend to gather, then work on boosting the cooler, less popular corners to lift the energy overall.

Hotspots

Mapping successes and failures

The health of your home's energy will express itself in the events that take place in your life. Smooth-flowing energy there brings easy success to all of your plans and projects. Blocked energy creates obstacles that slow down progress, while stagnant energy brings sickness. Failure also is a direct result of blocked energy.

Learn to watch the flow of energy in your home. The easiest way to do this is to watch how visitors and residents alike move within and around the house. Observe where residents tend to gravitate. Identify rooms that simply never get used. You may think that the dining room would be used most, but if the energy there is bad, you will find that you and your family members tend to eat elsewhere in the home or dine out at restaurants more often, and thus not coming home for meals.

Become sensitive to the energy in your home

You can get a very good idea about the flow of energy in each room by simply observing how often it is used. Where healthy energy accumulates is where all members tend to gravitate. This is an excellent way to develop sensitivity to the energy within your own home.

As a first step, entice family members towards the center of your house. If this is also the family or dining room, it will imbue the heart of your home with vital energy. It also will bring wonderfully good energy into your home.

Decoding the meaning of shapes

20

There are five basic shapes that influence the energy of spaces and these arise from their element associations.

- The **round** shape is very popular as it signifies gold (metal element).
- The **square** shape signifies relationships and the family unit (earth element).
- The **rectangle** shape signifies growth energy (wood element).
- The **triangular** shape signifies upward mobility (fire element).
- The **curvilinear** shape signifies fluidity (water element).

When you think about shapes, consider the layout of your home as well as the shape of individual rooms. To ensure a symmetry of energy, feng shui always favors regular as opposed to irregular shapes. Symmetry and balance are central concepts in feng shui so that, for a shape to be irregular or asymmetrical, implies that it is incomplete. Thus a full square is always better than one with a corner missing. Rectangles that are well proportioned are preferable to ones that are too narrow, which also suggests that part of the shape is missing.

A full circle is preferable to a half circle, which is why bay windows are inadvisable. Small irregularities in the corners of rooms cause irregularity of luck. The "Pa Kua"—and octagon—is also considered an auspicious shape, especially when used for dining and coffee tables.

Paint walls to emphasize the regularity of room shapes. **Rectangular** walls, which are higher than they are broad—without appearing incomplete—are particularly beneficial in east and southeast corners of the home since the shape here signifies growth and success. The rectangle is the shape of the wood element and wood suggests spring, the season of growth.

Perfectly **square** shapes, which belong to the earth element, are ideal for the dining room and the dining table since the earth element not only reflects the stability of grounding energy, it also stands for the mother. The energy of the square is balanced and auspicious for continued family harmony.

Round shapes denote the metal element and are suitable for the west and northwest. A perfect round patch created with clever paintwork on a northwest wall brings good luck to the family patriarch. Paint it in gold for luster and extra good-luck symbolism. Do not make it too large, though, since the round shape can be overpowering.

Making the most of your home's layout

Although regular shapes are better feng shui, many homes have some irregularities—such as a "missing" corner or a bay window. Still, there is much you can do to promote harmonious energy in your home by incorporating regular, auspicious shapes wherever possible.

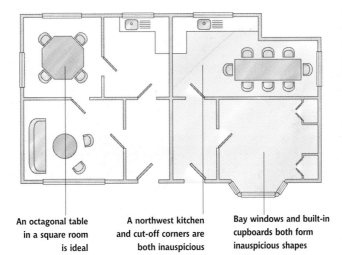

An octagonal table in a square room is ideal

A northwest kitchen and cut-off corners are both inauspicious

Bay windows and built-in cupboards both form inauspicious shapes

21   Secrets of the five elements

One of the great secrets of feng shui in the days before it became a household word was the principle of the five elements: water, wood, fire, earth and metal. These govern much of feng shui's principles. Today the theory of five elements is no longer a secret and many people who follow the Chinese esoteric sciences, including feng shui and fortune telling, the cultural arts such as kung fu and tai chi, as well as Chinese traditional medicine, are familiar with it.

All of these practices were based on the correct application of the five-element theory. The simplicity of this theory lies in the belief that literally everything in the Universe—from smells and tastes to colors, shapes, numbers, musical notes, directions, trigrams, symbols, seasons, body parts and organs, and so on—belongs to one of the five elements.

Harmonizing energy in your home

Assessing every item in your home according to whether it is water, wood, fire, earth, or metal will allow you to get a feel for which elements dominate the various parts of your home. This is the key to assessing your home's energy harmony. If you want to create powerful feng shui in the energy of your living space, then understanding the cycles and attributes of the five elements is the first step. Even people—based on their birth data and gender—can be defined according to these elements.

The five-element cycle

Assessing how the five elements are represented in your home helps you to understand its energy. The attributes of the five elements balance one another as shown below.

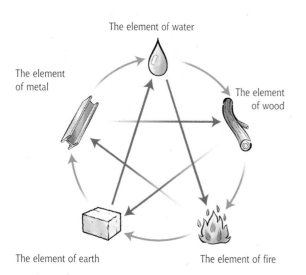

The element of water

The element of metal

The element of wood

The element of earth

The element of fire

Water

Plants represent the wood element

Earth

The metal element

Use the correct element colors for important rooms

22

Color is one of the easiest ways to bring harmonious energy into your living space. You can increase the power of feng shui in your home using the "Later Heaven Pa Kua". Almost all yang feng shui formulas depend on this arrangement of trigrams with eight sides. These reflect the eight compass directions, as well as their corresponding element and trigram. From these two attributes—element and trigram—it is possible to allocate different colors to each part of the home. The "Pa Kua" also helps you to use the most effective combinations of colors to enhance the energy in the most important rooms of your home.

The illustration shows which growth and resource colours (see the chart below) should be used at the different compass directions to gain your home the most beneficial effect.

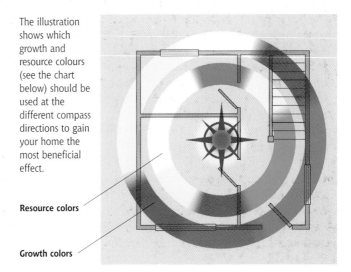

Resource colors

Growth colors

Using a compass

Stand at the center of your home and use a compass to find your orientations. By thinking of your home as one big space, you can mentally place the different rooms of your house into the sectors which equate to particular directions.

The important rooms of your home are your bedroom, your foyer area where the main door is placed, your dining room, your kitchen, your work/study area, and your living room. Depending on your lifestyle, different rooms will carry different connotations for you so you must also go with your own feelings when placing emphasis on rooms. For example, if you work from home and spend your day in your work/study area, it will be of particular significance to you.

Table of elements and colors for different room locations

Room location	Room element	Yin or Yang	Shade of color	Growth color	Resource color	Killing color	Exhausting color
North	WATER	Yang	Darker	**WHITE**	**BLUE**	YELLOW	GREEN
South	FIRE	Yin	Lighter	**BROWN**	**RED**	WHITE	EARTH
East	WOOD	Yang	Darker	**BLUE**	**GREEN**	WHITE	RED
West	METAL	Yin	Lighter	**YELLOW**	**WHITE**	RED	YELLOW
CENTER	EARTH	Both	Both	**RED**	**YELLOW**	GREEN	WHITE
Southeast	WOOD	Yin	Lighter	**BLUE**	**GREEN**	WHITE	RED
Northwest	METAL	Yang	Darker	**YELLOW**	**WHITE**	RED	YELLOW
Southwest	EARTH	Yin	Lighter	**RED**	**YELLOW**	GREEN	WHITE
Northeast	EARTH	Yang	Darker	**RED**	**YELLOW**	GREEN	WHITE

Yang and yin shades of color

To boost the energy in your important rooms with color therapy, be aware of yang and yin. The more white added to a color the more yang it becomes, while the darker the shade, the more yin it will be. Use the table shown above to choose the overall color scheme for each room in your home, and to decide on particular shades.

23 Empowering the main door

The main door of your home is where the powerful cosmic energy of the outer environment connects with and enters your home. All other doorways, entrances, and exits are secondary conduits of chi. It is very beneficial to pay special attention to the main door of the house if you want to enjoy continuous good feng shui.

Protect and enhance your entrance

While there are lots of ways to encourage good chi to enter through the main door of your home, all can be summarized in just two words—"protect" and "enhance". Most importantly, keep the foyer areas inside and outside well lit. If you can, it is also beneficial to display auspicious images near the vicinity of the door to empower it.

Traditional screening wall

In the old days the wealthy Chinese used to place a screening wall about three metres (ten feet) from the door, facing it. On this screening wall, they placed images of auspicious creatures, such as Gods of wealth, the nine dragons, or bright red peonies associated with the eight Immortals. All of these auspicious images were believed to attract fresh new cosmic chi into the home continuously.
You can employ the essence of this method near your own main door—perhaps including auspicious features in a front garden—referring to the plan opposite for ideas.

The main doors of domestic dwellings and businesses need brightly lit entrances to create good fortune feng shui.

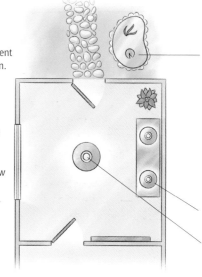

• Water is a powerful energizing element in a front garden.
• Vases create peace and harmony on an otherwise uncluttered side table.
• Bright lights encourage a flow of good chi to enter the home.

Water feature placed on the right side of the door will cause the man of the house to develop a roving eye. It's better to place water on the left of the door

Vase

Bright overhead light

Blocks outside the door hinder your success 24

Make sure that the energy flowing into your home is never blocked. Physical blockages easily translate into obstacles that prevent you from enjoying success in any of your endeavours. Furniture placed outside the door on verandas and patios should not encroach on the main door.

A winding path to the door
Any lane or path leading to your main door should be curved and preferably winding. A straight path that leads directly into the home sends in slivers of killing energy. The width of the path should stay constant, neither narrowing toward the house nor as it moves away from it. Placing lights on the pathway is auspicious.

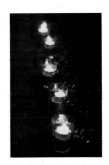

A winding path to the main door dispels killing energy along the way. To further enhance positive energy flow, place lit tealights along the edges of the path.

Allowing only good energy into your home 25

Keep the main door of your home in good condition. If hinges come loose have them repaired immediately. Such damage brings harmful energy into the home and, along with cracks on wooden doors or broken glass panes, signifies loss in your life.

Letting in fresh cosmic energy
The main door must not face a wall with a mirror on it, as this reflects away good fortune. Fresh cosmic energy cannot enter the home when it is confronted with a mirror, meaning that energy inside the home never gets revitalized. This is often a cause of illness and depression for residents. The main door should not open into a toilet or a staircase, or in a straight line with other doors inside the house. These features transform good energy instantly into harmful energy.

Ideally, the main door to your home will open onto a clear, light hall, and doors to other rooms will not face the main door directly.

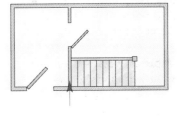

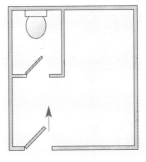

If the main door is opposite a door to a toilet then any fresh, positive energy that comes into your home will be converted into toxic energy.

26   Keeping the main door fully energized

Creating good energy around and near the main door is the first step in ensuring that only good energy enters the home. It is also beneficial to keep track of the changing energy patterns that afflict the main door from year to year.

Protective metal

Usually the presence of metal energy in the form of celestial guardians, such as a brass Chi Lin or brass Fu dogs, flanking the door offers strong protection against afflictive energies. It is also useful to install feng shui cures around the vicinity of the main door to ensure that your good feng shui is protected from year to year.

Good-fortune locations

First use a compass to locate the direction of the main door, then check the energy of this location for the coming year. In 2011, for example, you will have enjoyed good fortune if your main door is located in the northwest, and enhancing it with a water feature would be excellent. However, if your door is located in the east, you could suffer misfortune because the afflictive star here can cause money loss and accidents. In 2012, the good-fortune location for the main door moves to the west sector, and in 2013, good luck flies to the northeast sector of the home.

As such good-fortune locations and areas of affliction change from year to year, always be prepared to update your feng shui. Remember

A brass Fu dog flanking the main door acts as a guardian against harmful energy.

that these changes in chi energy begin at the start of the lunar New Year, on February 4. You will always find up-to-date information at www.wofs.com, which also carries an analysis of the annual changes in energy patterns that affect your main door.

Create space in the right places

27

The first step in creating a harmonious place in which to live is to define the space itself so that chi flows unimpeded into the home and settles and accumulates in auspicious areas. You need to create the best routes and resting places for the energy to move and gather. If your home is overcrowded with too much furniture, the removal of even a single piece can make all the difference.

It is a good idea to begin by taking stock of the overall arrangement of cupboards, chairs, and tables in your living space. This snapshot overview enables you to see how each room could benefit from having some space freed up to encourage

good-fortune energy to settle in all the right places of the home.

Attracting cosmic chi

Most often the best place to create some empty space for the chi to settle is deep inside a room. In the living area, for instance, the best place for chi to collect is the corner diagonally opposite the entrance door. This is an auspicious corner so that chi settling here before moving into other parts of the home will also be auspicious. To enhance the corner further after de-cluttering it, place just one lucky object here—cosmic chi will respond positively to its presence.

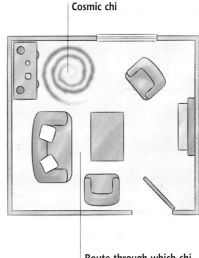

In a living room, chi gathers in an empty space diagonally across from the door before it flows into other parts of the living space.

Cosmic chi

Route through which chi can flow

Thoughtful spacing of objects in your living space provides chi with resting places and routes through which to move unimpeded.

28   Create meandering flows of chi in your home

When you arrange the furniture of your home create a mental image of traffic flow—how people will walk around objects—in your mind. Direct the traffic flow by placing pieces of heavy furniture in strategic places. Make sure the flow is meandering, and that family members will not be prone to walking into obstacles or corners. Disarm any sharp edges by placing softer items such as plants and sofas near them.

Softening the flow in strategic places
When more than two doors form a row where the flow of chi might gather pace, soften the flow by placing sideboards strategically so that the energy flows around them.

For a long corridor in the home, break the flow of energy by placing lights and decorative objects along its length. For a bedroom at the end of a long passageway, soften and slow down the flow of chi using lights and leafy plants.

ENERGY TIP

Visualizing flow

Place furniture, lighting, and plants to encourage the flow of chi to keep moving along passageways—but not too fast.

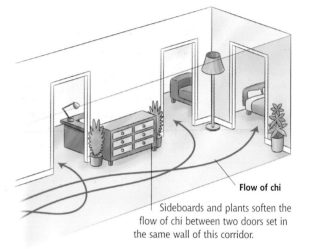

Flow of chi

Sideboards and plants soften the flow of chi between two doors set in the same wall of this corridor.

29   Generate pockets of concentrated energy

Create "pockets" of yang chi energy in every room to create good feng shui throughout the home. These pockets are special areas in which people regularly relax, eat, or engage in their favorite hobbies so that a concentration of energy builds up. In the living room you will need to arrange the furniture to create a pocket of yang chi whereas in the dining room this is usually formed naturally by meeting around the dining table.

The center of the house benefits most from a concentration of yang energy. If you find that this is not easily achieved in your home, place a television in the central room to generate a lively ambience. You want the heart of your home to be pulsating, alive, and active.

Seating areas naturally attract pockets of positive yang chi.

Chi pockets

Protruding corners send out killing chi

30

Sharp edges of walls and furniture are a source of bad energy. The remedy for this inside homes and offices is to place something directly in front of the protruding edge so that it is blocked from view. Camouflaged edges lose their unfriendliness and are transformed from being sources of bad energy into harmless structures.

Edges can also be made blunt so the sharpness of the edge disappears thereby losing their threatening energy. Stand-alone square pillars or exposed corners that are the source of misfortune energy can be made harmless this way. If you are on the receiving end of these edges you will tend to be more susceptible to illnesses and accidents. Blunt these edges by literally slicing off the sharp corner or, if they are pillars, wrap them with mirrors. This has the effect of making the pillar

Square glass tables such as these look so elegant, but create poison arrows due to multiple sharp corners.

merge with the rest of the room, thereby visually blunting the edges.

If you have already used these remedies, remember that these cures need to be renewed. Whatever is placed in front of sharp corners needs to be changed and renewed regularly. Over time remedies lose their strength and must be revitalized. I usually change my cures before every lunar New Year to ensure adequate strength to overcome hostile killing energy.

Pieces of furniture such as desks and sideboards also have edges that can create bad energy. In such instances, the solution is to rearrange the desk or cupboard so the edges do not cause a feng shui problem. When you rearrange your rooms, you are in effect moving the energy.

Positioning mirrors on pillars

Placing a mirror on square pillars as shown above helps to dilute poison arrows that can emanate from each sharp corner of the pillar, creating negative chi in the room.

31   Clearing blockages in the hallway

It is all too easy for clutter such as packages, newspapers, junk mail, raincoats, umbrellas, and so on to accumulate in the foyer area of your home. This is really the worst place to let clutter pile up, and it can happen so fast that you may only notice it when you start to look for the reasons why your luck has suddenly taken a turn for the worse.

Reversals of fortune

Frequently, I have gone to the homes of people who have suffered sudden reversals of fortune only to discover that the downturn in their lives or businesses has been caused by nothing more sinister that a blockage of energy. This blockage is usually near the main door, though sometimes it occurs in corners that would be bringing annual luck were it not for the piles of clutter suppressing the good fortune.

Bright, clean halls and foyers create excellent feng shui, allowing chi to meander and bring the inhabitants good fortune. When chi becomes inhibited due to clutter, misfortune can result.

Forming good habits

Make it a habit to keep the area just inside the home, as well as just outside the main door, clear of blockages. Keep plants and any other decorative objects in good condition, and don't let too many pile up.

It's fine to have some furniture in your hall to slow down chi, but don't let clutter pile up—display only a few decorative items.

Toilets near the front door bring a host of problems

32

If you have a toilet situated near the main front door—either immediately facing it or positioned on the next floor directly above the front door, so that it presses down upon it—good luck flies out of the home. This can make the family terribly unhappy, as there will be misunderstandings between the parents and between parents and children. They simply cannot live in peace and health when these afflictions make their presence felt. And when the chi energy of the year and month are harmful (see Tip 94) the afflictions become compounded and the situation deteriorates still further.

The location of a downstairs bathroom impacts upon the luck of your house.

Toilet remedies

The remedy for a badly located toilet is to keep the room's door closed at all times. Toilets located above the main door bring severe bad luck to the entire household and therefore, to counter the negative effects, you need to shine a very bright light up at the ceiling to symbolically lift the chi. However, if the affliction proves to be too excessive or severe, you might have no option other than to relocate the toilet to another sector of the home.

Toilet afflictions

Toilets that directly face the door cause all energy entering the home to become negative. And, depending on the direction of the toilet vis-à-vis the main front door, the toilet can affect different kinds of luck as follows:

- Wealth luck is afflicted when the toilet is Southeast of the door.
- Career luck is disturbed when the toilet is North of the door.
- Romance and love luck becomes non-existent when the toilet is Southwest of the door.
- Descendants luck is hurt when the toilet is West of the door.
- Patron luck is hard to come by when the toilet is Northwest of the door.
- The luck of the father is affected badly when the toilet is Northwest of the door.
- The luck of the mother is badly hurt when the toilet is Southwest of the door.

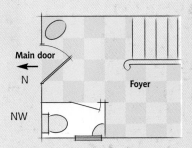

This toilet is located Northwest of the main door, which means you can have a hard time attracting patrons such as business investors or mentors.

- The health luck of residents is afflicted when the toilet is East of the door.
- The good name of the family is affected negatively when the toilet is South of the door.
- Study luck of the children is affected when the toilet is Northeast of the door.

33   Staircases that block success

A staircase's location can have a major impact on the energy of a home as it serves as a conduit of chi, transferring the energy from one level to another. The conduit must be positive and auspicious for good energy to prevail through all the levels of the home.

The best staircases are wide and curving. When gently curved, they encourage the flow of benevolent energy from one level of the house to the next. As straight staircases tend to take on the character of straight poison arrows it is always better to curve the staircase if possible. To energize straight staircases it is a good idea to keep them brightly lit and to hang happy pictures that have the effect of slowing down the energy, thereby transforming any tense energy into benevolent energy.

Solutions for staircases

If yours is a narrow staircase you should keep it well lit. Make sure that the steps have backs, and are not open; also, avoid steps with decorative holes as these weaken the energy, allowing it to seep away instead of moving up to the next level where it should be strengthened.

Metal staircases are best in the west and northwest, although concrete staircases are also good. Wooden staircases are best in the east and southeast as well as in the south. The idea is to select according to the element of the corner where the staircase is located. Staircases should not be in the center of the house—they are better by the side of the building.

Tips and remedies

Staircases should not start or end directly facing the following features or rooms:

A generous, sweeping staircase creates excellent feng shui in the home.

- A door
- A toilet
- A mirror
- The bedroom

as these are blocks to success. Of these taboos, the most harmful is when the staircase begins directly opposite the front door. Remedy this affliction by placing a bright light between the stairs and the door. Better still, block the door with a screen, forcing the chi that enters the house to meander before passing up the stairs.

Water under the stairs turns children into brats   34

A bamboo ornament will make children far less rebellious.

This is one of the worst features you can have in your home, as it is said to make any children living there endure misfortune. Water under the staircase, such as a toilet, fishtank, or miniature fountain, also causes them to become somewhat less than adorable—and transforms them into disobedient, rebellious brats. Water under the staircase will also bring long-term bad luck to the sons of the family. Whatever project or educational work they are involved in will suffer from unexpected setbacks, and they will meet with obstacles and troublemakers during their life.

Cures and talismans

It is best to stop using a toilet under the staircase, but as this is rarely practical, just keep the toilet door closed. Remove water features immediately and place a ceramic or gold pagoda in the vicinity of the staircase. The pagoda has a powerful, positive effect on growing children. In the old days, parents would even have their children wear a pagoda pendant to attract good study chi. You can also place an old jade or ceramic decorative bamboo plant in children's bedrooms to aid their concentration.

Staircase blues create miscommunication   35

There are different types of staircase, each one creating a unique flow of chi energy as it moves upward to the next level of the home. Take the following points into account when installing a staircase:

• The best staircase design is wide and curving, ideally wide enough for two people to pass.

• The staircase should look solid and not be open with holes between the stair risers.

• The staircase should not start or end directly facing a door, and especially not the main front entrance.

• A staircase should not appear to be "split" when it is near the main door—in other words, with a flight of steps going up and another flight of steps going down. This confuses the chi entering the home.

Staircases should turn softly and be decorated with airy, simple furnishings and art. Always keep the area well lit.

36 Long corridors cause problems with siblings

One of the most common causes of fighting and quarreling between brothers and sisters is due to bedroom location—when siblings' bedroom doors all open onto a long corridor. When this unfortunate arrangement occurs, too many "mouths" are created by the doors leading onto the corridor. Long, narrow halls are usually frowned on in feng shui, unless they are part of an outdoor veranda surrounding the house. When located inside the house, the longer and narrower the corridor is, the more harmful it becomes—especially when there are rooms off it as well as a room at the very end. People living in rooms opening onto such a corridor are likely to harbor animosity toward each other, especially those whose doors directly face each other in a confrontational manner.

Introducing distractions

As you are unlikely to be able to change the arrangement of doors, the cure for this situation is to create distractions in the corridor. You can do this by hanging art on the walls and introducing potted plants (if space allows), since this will cause the flow of chi to slow down. This is the correct way to transform chi from hostile to benevolent. When chi moves too fast, it is negative and harmful, bringing with it misfortune and bad luck.

Too many doors

Lots of doors leading off a hall or long corridor represent many mouths. In the case of siblings, this layout symbolizes everyone talking at once, leading to quarrels and disagreements. Use plants here to create some peace and quiet—they act to slow down overactive yang chi.

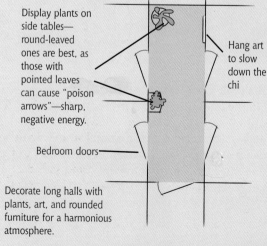

Display plants on side tables—round-leaved ones are best, as those with pointed leaves can cause "poison arrows"—sharp, negative energy.

Hang art to slow down the chi

Bedroom doors

Decorate long halls with plants, art, and rounded furniture for a harmonious atmosphere.

Creating feng shui strength in living rooms 37

The living room area is probably the best place to activate good feng shui by using symbolic decorative images. One of the joys of feng shui is that there are so many animals, flowers and other images available that are deemed to have an auspicious meaning.

Activating the eight aspirations
We all have many hopes and desires, and the Chinese have summarized them into eight main aspirations, as follows:

1 A loving and close family

2 Attaining career success

3 Good descendants

4 A good and respectable name

5 Enjoying good health

6 Knowledge and wisdom

7 Wealth

8 The protection of a powerful mentor

Each of these eight types of good fortune can be activated and strengthened using symbolic images that will enhance good feng shui. Images of auspicious animals have appeared in paintings, sculptures, porcelain, embroidery and carvings throughout the history of Chinese culture. This belief in lucky imagery has resulted in the wealth of wonderful decorative art we have inherited today from hundreds of years of Chinese artistry.

Auspicious objects create good chi
Simply decorating the living room with auspicious objects will usually create the chi energy that attracts the eight types of good fortune. Use the living room to showcase art and decorative objects featuring auspicious images, making sure that they are correctly placed to enhance the feng shui.

Animal images, such as the horse, are symbols of strength and good fortune.

Positioning art for positive benefits
Thoughtful positioning is particularly vital if you are placing decorative objects in corners of the room. Here, each object should reflect the element of the corner.

For example, in an earth corner of the southwest or northeast you might want to put an earth-based object such as a ceramic or crystal figurine of an auspicious animal. Remember that the luckiest corner is always diagonally opposite the door. Alternatively, if you hang up a mirror on a wall in the living room, make sure that it does not reflect the door—otherwise it will cause chi energy to fly out immediately.

38 Bright light always generates yang energy

As well as using art and decorative objects in the home to bring good luck, you can also harness the powerful yang energy of bright lights. A home is always luckier when the ambience is bright, without being glaring, than when it is somber.

Be sensitive to the moods created in your home by light. Soft or warm lighting—or indeed any kind of lighting that creates the ambience you feel most comfortable with—is fine so long as your home is never overly dark with lots of shadows. In the daytime your home will flood with the stimulating yang energy of the sun but, at nighttime, the darker, cooler yin energy from moonlight sets in.

Yin-yang balance at nighttime

While yin chi is suitable for the nocturnal hours, keep a good amount of yang energy flowing through your home as well. Remember that in yin there must always be a little bit of yang, and vice versa, as an excess of one or the other results in space that is not in balance and so cannot attract good fortune. This is why keeping the lights turned on through the night is such a good feng shui habit.

I keep the garden and porch lights on, as well as the altar lights and living room downlights inside as well. My main door foyer area is always kept lit as this part of the home benefits most from a continuous supply of yang chi energy.

39 Let natural sounds permeate your living areas

If you don't have animals to keep the atmosphere full of good yang energy, invest in pairs of dog or cat figurines as yang symbols.

The sounds of nature are a wonderful source of yang energy. Silent homes or rooms—suggesting the yin aura of tombs and underground places—are not at all conducive to activity and life. For homes to resonate with good feng shui, create features that emit natural sounds. The best include the sound of water flowing gently through a water feature, the sound of twinkling windchimes, or the rustle of leaves blown by fans.

When the home is empty all day

If the home stays silent through the daytime, especially when the whole family is out—perhaps husband and wife at work and kids at school—the atmosphere within will take on yin essence unless there is the sound of life. I am a great believer in keeping a pair of pet dogs or cats as these create "life essence" in the house. Alternatively, a workable solution is to keep the radio or television on while you are away from home.

Round dining tables result in harmonious meals

40

When it comes to selecting an auspicious dining table, it is useful to know that according to feng shui all the regular shapes are auspicious—square, rectangular, round, and even the octagonal Pa Kua shape. Each of the basic shapes also signify one of the five Chinese elements, and it is the square (Earth), rectangular (Wood) and the round (Metal) shapes that are best for dining tables. The Fire element shape is triangular, while the Water shape is wavy.

The harmonious circle

The Chinese have always had a preference for round dining tables, because this is the shape that make for harmonious meals. Family members quarrel and disagree less when the table is curved. A round table also has no sharp edges to disturb the harmony of the home. Indeed, it is rare to find anything but a round table in the dining rooms of Chinese homes—and the larger the table, the more auspicious it is deemed to be. In addition, these tables are almost always made of the finest woods and are either carved with a collection of auspicious symbols or engraved with four-season fruits,

A circular dining table symbolizes heaven chi and harmonious relationships.

plants, or flowers signifying auspicious abundance throughout the entire year.

The circle is also a special symbol signifying heaven chi. There is, thus, less possibility of energy becoming aggravating and the authority of the father figure is respected. Family members who sit together at a round table are deemed to be connected within a good relationship. To ensure good feng shui, individually and collectively, everyone should be allocated a seat around the table according to his/her best direction. Use the Kua formula of personalized good and best directions (see Tip 41) to maximize their luck each time they sit down to dine together. Select the nien yen, or family direction, for each person living in the house.

What's the element of your table?

A rectangular table symbolizes the Wood element.

A square table symbolizes the element of Earth.

A round table signifies Metal, the most auspicious feng shui table shape.

41 Sit in your nien yen direction for family harmony

Sit facing your nien yen direction for more family unity.

Find your nien yen direction

YOUR KUA NUMBER	YOUR NIEN YEN DIRECTION	EAST OR WEST GROUP?
1	South	East
2	Northwest	West
3	Southeast	East
4	East	East
5 *		West
6	Southwest	West
7	Northeast	West
8	West	West
9	North	East

* Those with Kua number 5: women read Kua 8, men read Kua number 2.

Sitting directions can create relationship woes when they are oriented to harm rather than benefit individuals. If you want to make the best of compass-formula feng shui to create happy, harmonious energy for everyone in the home, it is an excellent idea to learn the Kua formula. Once you have calculated your Kua number, you can determine your personalized family orientation. This is your nien yen direction. Facing this direction when you sit will bring harmony in all your relationships. It also ensures that the family unit stays happy and intact. Set a place for each family member around the dining table so that they each face their nien yen. Calculate your Kua number and determine your nien yen direction as follows:

Calculating your Kua number

Everyone's personal auspicious and inauspicious directions are based on gender and date of birth, and from these basic details you can calculate your Kua number. There are 9 Kua numbers altogether, each belonging to either the East or West group of directions. To find out your Kua number, follow these steps:

1 Take the last two digits of your year of birth and add them together until the result is a single digit. However, if you are born in January you need to make an adjustment for the lunar year and deduct one year from your year of birth before applying the formula.

2 Next, if you are male, deduct the number obtained from 10 and the result is your Kua number. If you are female, add 5 to the number to find your Kua number.

3 Reduce this number to a single digit if necessary. Example: for a female born in 1970:
  7 + 0 = 7; females add 5, so 7 + 5 = 12;
  1 + 2 = 3, so the Kua number is 3.

Golden rules for kitchen location

42

Feng shui gives important guidelines for siting your kitchen. Firstly, it is best located deep inside your home, although not in its center. If possible, the kitchen should not be visible from the front door so that, ideally, a wall will separate it from the front of the house. It is best sited on the ground floor, as a kitchen located at basement level brings bad luck to the family's matriarch. As you walk into the home, a kitchen on the right is far preferable to one on the left. Kitchens that are located on the left side of the house, looking in, tend to cause the siblings of the family to quarrel. They can also provoke children to fight severely with their parents.

Avoid the northwest and southwest
Do not site a kitchen in the northwest of your home as this damages the luck of the patriarch. Often it will cause him to lose his major source of success—be it a powerful benefactor, mentor, or patron. A kitchen in the southwest hurts the luck of the matriarch, causing her to lose power and status within

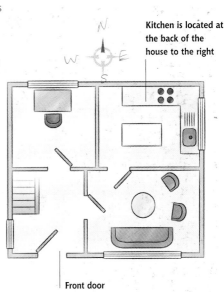

This floor plan shows an ideal location for a kitchen. As you walk in, the kitchen cannot be seen from the front door. It is situated on the ground floor, to the right at the back of the home.

Kitchen is located at the back of the house to the right

Front door

the family. In many cases, it causes the husband to take a mistress or even leave the home for a second marriage. Anything that afflicts the matriarch will also cause problems for the family.

Revitalizing salt rituals in kitchens

43

Of all the rooms in the home, the one most vulnerable to bad or stagnant energy is the kitchen. As this is where the family's food is cooked everyday, the energy of the kitchen can be transferred easily to every member of the family.

Once a year give the floor, door, and walls of the kitchen a salt wipe, a simple but powerful way to ensure that kitchen surfaces are clear of negative chi, and that food cooked in your kitchen never gets afflicted by harmful or stagnant energy.

To clean your kitchen with salt, press a damp cloth into natural rock salt and, as you wipe all the surfaces, visualize that you are drawing out the old, negative chi.

Always use natural rock salt because you need the power of the earth—synthetic salt is ineffective.

44 Managing fire and water elements

As you wash and cook food in your kitchen, be sensitive to the conflicting energies of the fire and water elements. Of all the elements, these have the potential to be most beneficial or harmful. Water brings wealth but can also drain it away. Fire brings a good name and reputation, attracting honor, fame, success, and recognition, but it can also burn everything to ashes. Water and fire provide the potential both for very good or very bad outcomes. Between the two, it is water that controls fire.

Locating the sink and stove

Water and fire confrontation is the cause of commotion and quarrels within the home so consider the location of the sink and stove in your kitchen, and do not have a toilet or water tank above the stove.

During the yin hours of the night, keep at least one light turned on in the kitchen to rekindle the fire energy. Symbolically, this will also keep the kitchen of the home warm, ensuring that yang energy never dies.

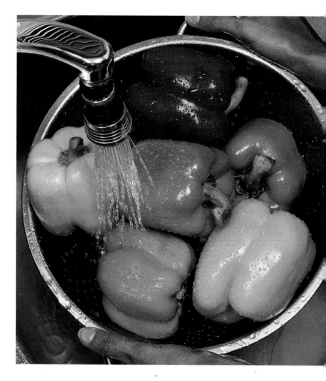

Inside your kitchen make sure that the water tap is not near the stove and does not directly face it. The stove symbolizes the fire element, which will react negatively to the water element.

ENERGY TIP

Siting the stove auspiciously

Avoid putting mirrors or mirror tiles above the stove as they will cause the fire energy to double, which is harmful. Also make sure the stove does not face a staircase, refrigerator, toilet, water pipe, store room, or door. Ideally, position it diagonally opposite the kitchen door. If it is then opposite a back door, put up a divider to block the energy flowing through the door. The stove should never be below a window.

Restful energy in the bedroom

Always underplay the presence of yang energy when decorating bedrooms. If there is too much yang chi in a bedroom, it will activate your mind and make it difficult for you to sleep well. If yin and yang are not in harmony, this will also result in restlessness. At nighttime, your bedroom signifies a place of security and sanctuary. It's best to choose soothing colors rather than stimulating ones. Neutral colors work a lot better than primary ones.

Avoid pictures of people

Try not to activate the bedroom with too many decorative objects. Keep celestial guardians and the dragon in the living areas and not the bedroom. It is also best not to hang photographs or paintings of people on bedroom walls. Some newly-weds like to hang their wedding photograph inside the bedroom, but this is definitely not recommended—it is far better to hang pictures of your loved ones in an energizing yang chi area.

Choose subtle lighting

In the bedroom yin energy should take precedence over yang energy, so keep lighting muted. A general rule is the older a bedroom's occupants, the softer the lighting should be. Lamps are best placed at the sides of the bed, not overhead.

Earth tones such as brown and cream work particularly well in a bedroom because the earth element is grounding and relaxing.

Keep decorative objects to a minimum in the bedroom. The aim is to create a tranquil environment that soothes the mind, allowing deep and restful sleep.

46 Confronting rooms lead to misunderstandings

When doors into bedrooms directly confront each other, there is certain to be misunderstandings between the occupants. This is one of the causes of sibling rivalry within families (see Tip 36). When daughters occupy rooms directly opposite each other, for example, the energy created will be one of hostile competition. This is particularly the case when one room door faces Southwest and the other faces Northeast—two earth chi directions confronting each other sets up a situation of intense rivalry.

Calming sibling rivalry

The cure for this situation is to install a bright light between the two doors. The light creates fire energy, which enhances the doors. Once there is sufficient resource chi created, the hostility evaporates. Bright lights also create precious yang energy, which is effective when the doors face other directions as well.

If sisters' bedroom doors are opposite one another, this can create intense sibling rivalry. Enhancing the hall with side tables and soft lighting can help calm hostile energy between the rooms.

PROJECT

Lighting the area around your children's rooms

If you do not have a ceiling light fitting close to the confronting doors of your children's bedrooms, you will need to find other ways to keep the hall area brightly lit to dispel irritations. You can place tables with lamps to the side of the doors, install small wall lights, or even hang fairylights or other decorative illumination around wall art and mirrors. Use an extension cord if you have to, but make sure anything electrical is safely installed and positioned where it can do no harm.

Activating creativity in work areas

Make a conscious effort to stimulate creative chi in the work areas of your home, especially if you work from a home office. In this case take advantage of the fact that the arrangement and décor of your office is entirely under your control.

Most importantly your work space must benefit from plenty of yang energy, which stimulates your vitality as well as your creativity. Yang energy requires the office to be well lit and have the benefit of natural sounds such as the rustling of leaves or the flow of water from a miniature water feature.

Benefiting from primary colors

A burst of energizing color activates the space, and may come from a flower arrangement, a piece of art, or a well-chosen shade of paint. A good dose of a primary color is excellent as it has not been diluted with other shades and is entirely yang in energy. Avoid somber colors in your home work area as they are likely to dull your energy.

While it is good to include features that stimulate your senses, keep a balance. It is helpful to try to

Yang energy must be activated, so your work space should be airy and well lit. Keep clutter to a minimum.

include objects that represent all five elements through the room. Once your work area is full of positive chi, you are certain to be rewarded with a great many new and creative ideas.

48 Ensuring mental clarity in study areas

Children who have started at school, as well as teenagers attending college, need a corner where they can study effectively. Ideally, this corner will enable them to study facing their best self-development direction—known as the Fu Wei direction. This enhances their concentration and enables them to develop mental clarity.

To work out the correct direction for your child to face in, you first need to calculate his or her personal Kua number (see Tip 41) then use the table below, which is based on the lunar year of birth. This determines which of the eight primary and secondary directions brings concentration during study and the best exam luck.

A table with a smooth, flat surface forms an ideal work space. Plenty of daylight will enhance the area with stimulating yang energy.

ENERGY TIP
Creating a perfect workspace for your child

Ideally your child's workspace should not be in their bedroom where the different energies associated with restful sleep and study might clash. If this is not possible ensure that they keep any papers on the desk to their left to simulate dragon chi—papers in front of them might block their work and piles of work directly behind them might make them feel weighed down with the stress of examinations. Also ensure that their computer is turned off before they go to sleep and, ideally, is covered up.

The table below gives the best, or Fu Wei, direction for a child to face while doing schoolwork or studying for examinations.

KUA	1	2	3	4	5	6	7	8	9
Best direction	north	SW	east	SE	*	NW	west	NE	south

* If the child is male, the direction is southwest and if female the direction is northeast.

The right desk helps bring success

To enhance your child's study area, it also helps to choose a suitable desk or table. Its surface should be level, and there should be nothing about it that your child finds disconcerting or awkward. Seek your child's opinion on this. For example, do not choose a desk that has an overhanging set of drawers or cupboard. The best work desk is larger than the normal standard-size desk seen at school. In fact the larger the desk the better, as this increases your child's success.

To stimulate mental clarity place a quartz crystal, with a single point, on the desk. Encourage your child not to let the crystal absorb other people's energy. He or she should place it on the desk while studying and carry it into the examination hall as a good luck charm.

An eight-step revitalizing program

49

Once you have mastered the feng shui basics, give yourself time and space to revitalize your home.

1 Begin by making a list of all the things that are needed. Start with your own mind and inertia will fly out the window. Motivate yourself by visualizing your home with fresh energy that is clean, clear, and auspicious. Give yourself a time frame for this. Decide to do it all in one weekend or over four weekends, allotting yourself different rooms for different weekends.

2 Get organized. Spend ten minutes in each room with a notebook. List the things that need changing in every room, all the clutter you want cleared, and all the repair work you want to initiate. When you are finished, list the rooms in order of importance. Assign other members of the family to rooms if you want them to become involved or assign yourself a day to address each room.

Getting started

3 Here's a tip: Start with the room that is of least importance to you, and leave the room that is most important until last. This way, you are sure to finish the job.

4 Convert one of your bedrooms into a workroom. This will be a halfway house room for you to place all the stuff you want to give away, repair, and sell.

5 Buy trash bags—ensure that they are strong and large, as you must throw into them all the things that you don't want. Clearing clutter is really very therapeutic—and it gets easier with practice. Do not cause yourself stress by being indecisive about what to keep and what to throw away. When in doubt, keep it. It will get junked in the next round of clearing in six months' time. Also, as you become better at this, you will find yourself becoming increasingly non-attached to possessions. Clearing clutter is not a one-time thing. Over time, you will find yourself doing it regularly—perhaps once or twice a year.

6 Revitalize your house with a fresh coat of paint at least once every three years. Get professionals in to do this if you can afford it. If not, then make a fun DIY (do-it-yourself) day of it. Paint your home room by room. Have fun with colors (see Tip 22) but if in doubt use white, which is very yang and suitable for all rooms. Give your home a proper scrub before you begin painting. Think of the layers of negative energy being scraped away and replaced with fresh new energy. The smell of fresh paint alone will make you feel better.

New light and air

7 This is one of the most effective ways to revitalize the energy of homes. Invest in a few extra lights—new lampshades, uplights, and light washes—and you will be amazed at how much warmer and brighter the energy in your house feels. Bring in sunshine energy with window crystals. Wash your curtains and hang faceted crystals in windows in order to draw in sunshine energy. It is very good to give your home or apartment a sunshine bath during the summer. Sunshine has the power to revitalize everything in your home—the walls, furniture, pillows, cushions, beds, carpets, and curtains. Sunshine energy brings fresh new yang energy into the home.

8 Let the wind flow through your house. Chi rides the winds. Bringing in the gentle breeze is inviting precious new chi into the home. It is therapeutic and very revitalizing.

50   Dejunking your life when you have moved on

It is amazing how much junk we collect. Our homes, and lives, collect it constantly. So does the mind. Junk-thoughts intrude upon our minds all the time. Try focusing on silence for a minute and you will see how hard it is. Thoughts flit in and out of the mind all the time—random thoughts enter our consciousness from various compartments of the memory bank, as if the brain is a machine running on automatic. It is the same with the home; in every corner of every room, there are random objects—articles of all kinds, small things, big things, fun things, useful things, junk things—that annoy and create stress for us. Our untidy rooms, stuffed closets, and piled-up desks can be so stressful. Usually we don't notice them, but, once we try to move on, or the thought of wanting to move on takes hold of us, the junk in our lives starts to overwhelm us—and often distracts and irritates us. Material and non-material junk is created by the mind.

Clutter is subjective–and books are a prime example. Giving away books you no longer want or need frees you from old ideas that may be holding you back.

Why clutter is subjective

Deciding whether something is junk is a purely subjective decision. Someone's prized possession is another person's junk. Something that means a great deal to someone else can mean absolutely nothing to you. So, dejunking your life means getting rid of stuff that you think of as junk. You are the one who must define what is junk.

Keeping precious items

Everything that gives you joy, makes you laugh, and inspires you—for whatever reason—is precious to you as it brings nourishing energy. Surrounding yourself with things you love, and which have meaning for you, will always strengthen you as the energy that vibrates around such objects is synchronized with your own.

Discarding bad-memory junk

Everything that causes you pain or anguish, makes you stressed out, annoys you, makes you feel inadequate, brings back unhappy memories, dulls your brain, and simply tires you out—in any way at all—is junk. All of it should be cleared and thrown away, never to annoy, disturb, or cause you stress ever again!

So when you have tired of anything—whether it is a book, newspaper, bag, clothes, decorative object, painting, furniture, curtains, or anything at all—however big or small, worthless or valuable, and it has lost its special meaning for you, lost its glitter... throw it out, sell it, or give it away!

Clutter that blocks energy

51

If you want your life to flow smoothly, clear everything that obstructs the flow of energy into and inside the home. Blocked energy vibrations of the home have a negative effect on its residents' well-being. Energy should move unimpeded from the entrance into the home and from one room to the next. When energy is blocked, your life becomes blocked—life becomes a struggle and success is hard to come by.

Where to begin
The foyer, hall, and staircase areas are most susceptible to clutter buildup. They are the home's energy conduits, so it is vital to keep them clutter-free.

The foyer
Blocked foyers create a hostile environment whose bad energy permeates through the rest of the home, so clear this precious space of shoes, overcoats, and umbrellas. This allows the

energy that enters by the main door to settle and accumulate before traveling through the rest of your home. Place a small side table here to hold everyday junk, and clear out your foyer daily. Keep walls and floors clean and uncluttered, and discard any tired paintings, posters, and other decorative objects. When you have created a clear, welcoming path through the foyer, vibrant good fortune chi can enter your home without hesitation.

Corridors and small halls
These areas move the energy from room to room. Sure places to attract the buildup of clutter are sideboards, closets, and tables, where magazines, newspapers, junk mail, and forgotten unimportant possessions tend to get dumped. Clear these away. I am amazed at how fast junk piles up on tabletops and countertops. This type of clutter can be harmful when it piles up in halls and blocks the flow of chi. The solution for this is to move the furniture away, thereby creating a smooth path through which the chi can flow. Place a wastepaper basket here instead!

Staircases
These move the energy from one level of the home to the next, so they should not be stacked with clutter. Keep your stairways clutter-free, so that the flow of chi into the living quarters of the home is smooth. This greatly facilitates the replenishment of chi throughout the home.

Using Mirrors
Mirrors in halls or corridors should not reflect clutter as, symbolically, this doubles the negativity of junk. Use a rounded side table or closet to keep junk at bay; a round-leaved plant helps the smooth flow of chi at the corner of the alcove.

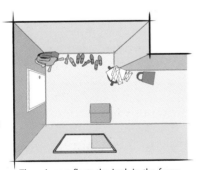

The mirror reflects the junk in the foyer.

The mirror doubles the good chi of a junk-free foyer.

52   Clearing clutter awakens chi

Clearing clutter is the best antidepressant there is. This is because stale, stagnant air that usually sticks to untouched, unmoved junk in the home often makes the surrounding chi heavy, creating vibrations that make you feel depressed. Each time I meet someone assailed by the blues who seems set on a downward spiral of depression, I know that part of the reason is that the energy of their surrounding space is too heavy for them and is weighing them down.

Beating the blues
Making the effort to awaken the chi of their living space by moving stuff around—not necessarily junk, but just stuff that has somehow piled up over the years—is usually so effective in forcing their own internal chi to also move that the result is a lifting of their spirits that is amazing to watch and experience. A certain lightness of being begins to pervade the atmosphere, not unlike the effect that an hour's work-out at the gym has. Clearing clutter engages both the physical and mental dimensions of the self. It is hard work physically, but it is also very relaxing. As all those trash bags pile up, it is as if, in freeing the chi around you, you are also lifting your own spirits. Depression flies right out of the window and, as you finish your clear-out, a genuine sense of renewal comes over you.

Clearing clutter and storing what you keep effectively brightens the chi of your home.

53   Attuning to the clearing process

It is important to attune yourself to the clearing process. The act itself is a departure from a normal kind of day. It is a departure from routine, and the mind gets a creative jolt that is not unwelcome. When the mind focuses on the process of dejunking physical space, it automatically goes into cleansing mode.

This means that what you do in the material space around you often imprints itself on the subconscious mind as well, so that tuning in to the clearing process creates many wonderful side effects. This is not just shrugging off garbage from your life and mind in a subconscious way, but also the mind goes into an organizational mode. There is an instant when the mind tunes into what can be done to simplify the cleansing process in the future and a certain awareness of space takes root.

Every time you clear out your clutter, it will take you less time to do so and the whole process will feel increasingly natural. Each time it will become easier, but the important thing is to start, for, once you experience its benefits, you will want to do it again and again. This is how the mind reacts, adapts, and contributes to any beneficial activity.

Not all clutter is bad

Distinguish good memorabilia from bad: think about what kind of memory an object evokes, rather than accepting it as a part of your personal history. Hold on to the good memories.

There are things in your life that you simply have no more use for, yet they continue to hold a small place in your heart—for whatever reason. These are things you are not yet prepared to let go of. In these cases, be soft on the so-called clutter—keep it, if only for another season, or until such time as you are ready to let go of it. News clippings of some past success, a faded picture of a long ago time, an old school report card, a birthday wish sent by some long-forgotten admirer whose words you loved, a childhood notebook, a lace blouse that brings back memories of good times—anything at all that would be thrown away under normal circumstances but which you still want—there is nothing and no one stopping you from keeping it. The object may be of no value, yet something holds you back from getting rid of it. Keep it, then, and realize that not all clutter is bad.

Trash or treasure?
There are always simple, even silly, objects in our lives that continue to carry positive energy simply by virtue of what they mean to us—happiness chi clings to things just as strongly as unhappiness chi. Energy works equally well either way. There is also a time dimension to energy. Who can say when something of great sentimental value becomes merely junk?

So accept that not all clutter is bad. There is no need to treat it like junk either. Honor things that once gave you joy. You will find that the memory of a moment of courage actually brings you courage when you need it, just as the memory of a moment of triumph can be intensely uplifting. There is no need to throw away objects that trigger such positive memories, which are reinforcements for our happiness.

55 First clear out the real junk: unwanted stuff

Every home has its fair share of unwanted stuff—things that no member of the family wants, yet which no one gets around to throwing away. In this category of clutter are the obvious newspapers and out-of-date magazines, catalogs, and junk mail. There is also the less obvious clutter, and this is what can cause the energies of the home to fall out of sync, attract negative energy, or, worse, make energy stagnate and grow stale.

Here we are referring to electronic implements that can no longer be used, such as broken-down stereo sets, radios, computers, irons, kettles, and air conditioners. Many people simply cannot accept that these conveniences of the modern age—what are generally referred to as white goods—do have a limited lifespan and do not last forever. When they break down don't keep them in the hope they may be repaired—throw them away or, if possible, recycle them.

Old furniture, pictures, and electrical goods such as radios can be real junk. If they are not of true sentimental value and, importantly, do not work, discard them immediately.

Dealing with Hoarders

My husband kept his 1966 stereo system for years after it stopped working. He insisted on keeping an old refrigerator that had served us for twelve years, long after it had broken down. His closets were chock-full with suits and sports shirts bought decades ago. It is no wonder that his life went into a severe tailspin.

I decided to throw caution to the wind—and threw away all his hoarded junk. Interestingly, because what I cleared out was real junk, he never missed anything. That was the start of our good years. After that day, I systematically threw out everything that did not work, and renovated my home each year, corner-by-corner. I forced out all the junk that had piled up at the back of the house, in storerooms, and even in and around the outside bathroom.

This constant renovation allowed in precious new yang energy, as the throwing out of junk got rid of yin energy. Our life together just got better and better after that. We have been together now for over 35 years and he has accepted my fierce determination to throw out junk each year.

Indeed, once I realized how absolutely exhilarating this renewal process is, I began to look forward to clearing out our obviously unwanted belongings every year. I do this just before the lunar New Year, and I never cease to be amazed at the sheer volume of rubbish we manage to amass—and this is in spite of the clearing away I do each month. Newspapers, magazines, used batteries, and old clothes I sell to the junk man, who comes by regularly and pays us a few dollars for all our old possessions.

Clear junk that blocks doors and doorways 56

Keep entrances on both sides of doors free of junk, and good fortune chi will flow unimpeded into your life. Projects will move along smoothly, and relationships will bring you the joy associated with smooth sailing.

Types of door affliction

The doorway is where you, your spirit, and the spirit of your space and home move in and out. This flow of chi must never be blocked, afflicted, or tainted.

Blocked flow-paths

If this flow-path is blocked, your life also is blocked. Nothing works, nothing moves. Relationships flounder. People get stuck in ruts in their jobs. Upward mobility comes to a halt. When the path into the home is blocked, opportunities dry up. When the path from the home to the outdoors is blocked, you become imprisoned inside your home. Your social life dries up. You lose vitality, vibrancy, and energy.

Afflicted entrances

This happens when junk piles up to the extent that it poisons the energy of the doorway. Entrances

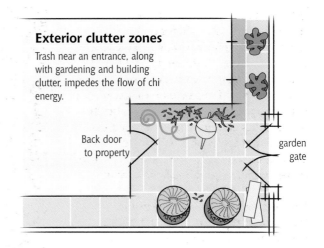

Exterior clutter zones

Trash near an entrance, along with gardening and building clutter, impedes the flow of chi energy.

Back door to property

garden gate

afflicted in this way may cause the home's residents to suffer illness, lose money, and experience one piece of bad luck after another.

Allowing the entrances of your home to become afflicted is akin to being attacked by poison arrows. It is absolutely vital to get rid of the source of this kind of affliction: clean both sides of the door, and clear away the junk near it.

Protecting Your Door from Tainted Energy

An entrance may be tainted by energy that has slowly piled up and turned poisonous through the passage of time, or by energy that has been brought in via incoming furniture, people with bad feelings, or objects brought in innocently by residents.

Entrance ways are especially vulnerable to incoming negative energy, and it is for this reason that feng shui experts always recommend placing the images of protective celestial creatures near them.

Because of this, you will find that many Chinese abodes even today place Chi Lins, Fu dogs, Pi Yaos (illustrated here) and even traditional door gods at the entrances of their homes. These are thought to

offer a certain amount of protection against incoming negative energy. If you have these protective symbols in your home, do make certain they are never overwhelmed by a pile of clutter around them.

In the past I have visited a number of shops and other businesses whose protective Fu dogs, positioned to guard the doorways, were literally buried under a pile of boxes and other junk. The owners wondered why their suppliers were cheating them. However, as soon as their entrances were cleared of all the rubbish that had piled up, their problems with their suppliers immediately cleared as well.

57   Remove junk obstructing corridors and halls

Make a special effort to ensure that the careless buildup of junk never blocks the halls and corridors of your home. These are vital conduits of chi flow and it is really important to let the chi move unobstructed through these areas. One way to guard against the buildup of junk is not to place tables or sideboards in hallways and corridors. By making sure that there are no convenient tabletops and storage spaces here, you will be helping these vital conduits of energy to stay tidy and clear. Think of corridors and staircases as the veins and arteries of your body, making precious energy flow inside you.

To help the flow of chi through every part of your home, it is always a good idea to keep hallways

Halls need good energy flow, but the chi must meander rather than rush. Placing an item of furniture, or an inspiring picture, at the landing helps the chi pause and create a calm and unhurried ambience.

well-lit and both the walls and carpets there clean. Most of the time, these places do not have access to natural light so make a conscious effort to ensure that the chi there does not become stale by leaving on a light.

Using Light and Music

Some time ago, I visited someone who lived alone in a London town-house. Her home felt very narrow and constricted. Directly facing the entrance door to her home was a staircase, with a long, thin hall running to the side of it. This hall—deep, dark, and gloomy—was also blocked by a coatrack which stood by the stairway. It seemed as if the many coats hanging off it had been there for a very long time. In fact, it gave me the creeps.

Now the owner suffered from severe loneliness. She had attended one of my lectures and something about her air of resignation, and her defeated expression, had tugged at my heartstrings. I had agreed to look at her home and it was clear to me that something could easily be done to bring back vitality into this lady's life. She was agreeable when I suggested that she throw away the cumbersome coat-rack, as well as the coats. She had long outgrown them, yet even through the change of seasons, it had never occurred to her to pack them away. Now she donated them to the local charity and immediately felt a rush of exhilaration

from having liberated the hall. Next, she brightened the whole foyer area by installing lights. She also placed a loudspeaker there to enhance yang energy with piped-in music, as I told her that this was one excellent way to attract more people into her life.

That was several years ago. The last time I met her, she was working part-time for a local Buddhist meditation center. Her social life has become very busy and her life has taken on new meaning. She looked so radiant and fulfilled.

Keep your kitchen clear as all junk there is bad 58

The buildup of junk in the kitchen can be quite dangerous. This is because bad energy can seep into the food you eat. Cooked food is not as susceptible to absorbing yin chi (which can cause illness) as cold food is, since it is already yin. If you are a salad-and-sandwiches person, do ensure that your kitchen stays reasonably free of yin energy, which emanates from kitchen clutter.

Revitalizing your kitchen

You need to dejunk your kitchen as often as possible to avoid this harmful build-up of yin chi. Below are essential practices:

Clean the refrigerator Do this once a month, so that leftover food does not get lost in the back of it and rot into poison. Do the same for the cabinets that hold grocery goods. For instance, people have a nasty habit of ignoring canned food for so long that it turns bad before they notice. The same thing happens with exotic sauces and seasonings that become harmful junk as they degenerate in half-open bottles and containers.

Check out cookware In the kitchen, all physical junk is bad and should be thrown away. Included in this category are not merely stale food and foodstuffs, but also broken plates, cups, and bowls. Cooking pots and pans also cannot last forever and, once defective, they should be replaced; don't buy a new frying pan and keep the old one with its scratched Teflon surface, or that worn-out, ugly coffee maker that you have already replaced with a brand new model.

Double-check trash cans So make sure to clear the garbage regularly and to throw away rotting food. Also, clear the cat litter and make sure that kitchen goldfish bowls are kept clean. I have seen untidy, dirty kitchens ruin more marriages and cause more heartache than I care to tell. Among all the rooms of the home, this is the place that is most vulnerable to the buildup of yin energy, so treat all physical junk here as bad and get rid of it.

A truly clean and well-ordered kitchen keeps energy-sapping yin chi at bay.

59   Treat bedrooms as sacred spaces

Keep your bedroom free of clutter for peaceful, restful sleep. Treat this area as if it is a sacred space, since this is where you spend all of your sleeping, subconscious time. It is where you leave the conscious world, and go into another dimension. Here is where you dream dreams, and let yourself go. Here is where you rest, cocooned from the world. So keep this space sacred and special.

Keep the energy of the bedroom free from energy that is negative, harmful, stale, or hostile—so throw out things that make the energy turn sour. Instead, place only things you love in your bedroom, things that make you feel pampered and beautiful.

Keep the bedroom bright, clutter-free, and comfortable.

Practical Tips

1. Don't store clothes high on elevated shelves in your bedroom. This is a bad idea because they create heaviness above the sleeping level. Store your winter wardrobe in a store-room and keep all of your suitcases in another room.

2. Keep all exercise equipment, bikes, and wall mirrors out of the bedroom. Your place of rest is not your gym.

3. Make sure that all work-related junk is kept away from the bedroom. Do not have a work desk here, so that you eliminate the danger of work-junk piling up inside the bedroom. Keep computers and telephones out. Let children have a special study room, rather than a desk in their bedroom. If there are insufficient rooms in your house for this, try to place the desk a little away from the bed so that junk that builds up on the desk does not affect the sleeping child.

4. Keep all dirty clothes inside a laundry basket. Nothing is more yin than dirty clothes, and the energy permeates any room pretty fast.

5. Do not place junk under, over, or beside a bed. Keep beds clean at all times.

6. Keep all doors clear of junk so that they open and close smoothly.

7. Never hang questionable art on the walls of your bedroom. Refer to the section on art to make certain you never hang anything that can attract bad luck.

8. Keep windows clear of clutter. Curtains can be left open or closed at night, but it is advisable to let the light flow in once the sun shines. Nothing brings in better yang energy than morning sunlight.

Clutter-clearing and cleansing of the bed space　60

I encourage all couples to undertake regular, systematic space cleansing of their bed. Start by clearing out all the clutter under the bed. It is vital to throw out the junk, no matter how sentimental you may be about the things kept there.

In the old days, when banks did not exist, many families literally slept with the family gold under the bed in the belief that this would safeguard their assets. A symbolic bowl of coins is therefore considered auspicious, as are crystals—often referred to as the treasures of the earth—under a bed. However, be cautious about which treasures are suitable to be stored here. Never place old clothes, books, albums, files, or personal memorabilia under a bed. Those with genuine value should be placed inside a gold box in a higher place. The symbolism of sleeping above personal items that are closely associated with you will press down your good luck. Photographs of your children placed under your bed will hinder their growth and development. Sleeping over photographs of the family breadwinner will similarly press down on their luck.

Keeping the underbed area clutter free safeguards you from sleeping over photographs or items that you associate with important family members, which symbolically presses down on their luck and afflicts the family.

Activating good fortune

It is also useful to regularly do a cleansing ritual of the bed space with incense and a singing bowl once a month. This will activate good fortune for your family. When the energy of the marital bed is systematically cleansed of negative energy, the chi does not have a chance to grow stale or die. This ensures that "family luck" remains vibrant and energized.

At the same time, it is important to get rid of all killing energy caused by secret poison arrows. These emanate from the sharp edges of walls and furniture and also from harmful heavy structural beams. Killing energy, or shar chi, poses immediate threats to a home's residents. Negative energy is also harmful, but its effect is less pointed and experienced over a longer period of time. Although both should be cleared, killing energy intensifies any danger to relationships, especially those of couples.

When the bed is afflicted by killing energy, there is no goodwill possible between the couple sharing it, and all their interactions will move their relationship progressively downhill. There definitely will be no descendants' luck. Even if they already have children, their family will not feel like a unit. Personally, I feel that the absence of good family luck is the saddest of all feng shui afflictions.

61 Purification procedures for your sleeping area

Prepare a jug of purifying saffron water to cleanse the space your bed occupies. It should be placed in a container specially designated for this purpose. After saffron has been soaked in warm water for a while, it turns the water yellow. Use the best quality saffron you can find—the best form of it comes from Greece; a few strands in a jug of warm water is all you will need. Also at the same time this, either in powder or block incense form. Saffron water and incense are really excellent for cleansing the bedroom, especially the area around the marriage bed.

Saffron is a very powerful substance for purifying space. It is used in many Taoist cleansing rituals, and features prominently in Hindu and Taoist puja ceremonies as well. In these rituals, saffron water is

Saffron is a traditional purifier used ritually in Eastern cultures.

used to symbolically cleanse the body, mind, and speech of devotees participating in the puja. Saffron is considered one of the most potent of purifying agents.

Also, it complements the feng shui arrangements already in your bedroom, and has the power to cure all afflictions caused by the monthly and annual Flying Stars that affect it. So you should be able to use it with confidence. The best thing about incense and saffron cleansing is that, while it diffuses negative chi, it does no harm to anything positive or auspicious.

The Saffron Ritual

This saffron and incense cleansing ritual can be done once a month. It takes only five minutes and is very powerful.

First, walk three times around the bed in a clockwise direction, allowing the smoke from the incense to waft over it. Next, create an invisible cocoon of protection around it by sprinkling the saffron water as you walk around it three more times.

Discard junk in storerooms, attics, and basements

62

Clearing clutter only becomes a complete exercise when you systematically begin to discard all the junk that lies hidden in storerooms, attics, and basements.

Four types of junk to let go of
You will find much that should be thrown away in these natural storage areas of the home. Below are four areas to begin with—so tune your mind into letting go of junk, and make a start.

Junk collections
These range from the sublime to the ridiculous—fans, plastic ducks, matchbooks, toy monkeys, carved horses, ceramic toads, stamps, and stones. Almost every kind of collection mania you can think of has been enjoyed by someone somewhere. If you have a collection that is no longer on display in your living room, and has found its way into your attic or basement, you have moved on. These objects no longer mean much to you, so why not arrange for them to go to someone else who will enjoy them? Kept in storage rooms, their energy simply stagnates.

Books and magazines
These make the energy of a room grow very stale, as they represent dated information—so discard immediately.

Photographs
Take some time to go through this third kind of junk. Throw away any images that don't bring back pleasant memories and definitely get rid of those that recall negative emotions. Keep only photographs that bring a smile to your face, not tears to your eyes. Then remount them. Give them fresh new energy so that they become a source of strength and love for you. Photographs are very much a part of your family so transform the ones that you keep into things that are genuinely precious.

If it's broken and not collectable, it's junk.

Broken equipment
Everything in the basement that is broken or has been discarded should be junked. Get rid of it all—stereos, TV sets, old computers, exercise equipment, hair dryers, lawn mowers, odds and ends for the car, plus all boxes, bottles, and other containers for which you have no need.

It is impossible to list everything that should be discarded from your storage rooms. In everyone's life there are things such as unwanted presents, things we dislike, and things that no longer work that we keep, out of misguided feelings of guilt or in the hope that they can be repaired some time. But, believe me, if you don't like it today, or don't need it today, chances are you will never like it or need it.

Turning Over a New Leaf
My father's collection of National Geographic magazines, lovingly bound over the years, choked my mother's energy long after he had died, Each time she spied them on the shelves, they would make her so remorseful that the only solution was to help her make a clean break with them. It was not until I had separated her from them that she recovered from the spiral of depression that had gripped her and regained her vitality.

63 Keep your work desk clear of junk

Your work desk should be kept reasonably clear of junk. If yours is a working style that requires piles of files and papers on your desk, then at least make certain that the mountain of files and paper is not placed directly in front of you, blocking your view. This will only cause your view of work itself to become blocked. Do not place piles directly behind you either, as this means you will always feel weighed down with work. Instead, keep files and papers to your left in order to simulate dragon chi.

Clear out your drawers

Desk drawers also have a way of becoming clogged with a broad variety of things that cross a working person's daily life at the office. Do not let these things choke up your career. A congested desk will create traffic jams in your working life. Instead, keep the chi moving, especially the chi on your desk. Let nothing stagnate. If you have fresh flowers on your desk, for instance, change the water daily and throw out wilting flowers, as there can be nothing more damaging to your working life than dying blooms.

Always keep any decorative items on your desk to a minimum. Framed photographs, crystals, pen holders, feng shui enhancers, and so forth, should all be kept to a sensible number. If these things threaten to overwhelm the tabletop, there is no space left for new opportunities to come in.

If you work at an antique desk, it is probably full of yin energy which will have you falling asleep in your chair. Cleanse it by rubbing it with rock salt to create positive yang energy and good concentration as you work.

You may keep your desk free of clutter, but be aware of shelves taking the strain. Their edges also create "poison arrows", a type of negative chi.

Keep books, diaries, and files to the left of your chair to activate energetic dragon chi.

Women should keep important items in the left-hand drawer.

Men should keep important items in the right-hand drawer.

Rearrange your décor at frequent intervals 64

One of the simplest yet most effective feng shui secrets I picked up many years ago when I lived and worked in Hong Kong was the great benefit of regularly rearranging furniture in the home. This encourages chi energy to move, preventing it from becoming stagnant. You do not even have to rearrange the furniture if you like it as it is—just moving it a foot from the wall to give the whole room a good clean then moving it back again will force the chi energy to move. Rearranging furniture is particularly beneficial because it re-channels the patterns of chi energy, reflecting its dynamic nature and attracting new cosmic energy into your home.

Annual rearranging and renovation

I usually rearrange my furniture at least once a year. I often move entire sets of furniture from one room to the next, and I even move the pictures hanging on the walls around to different rooms as well. This gives the house a new feel and energy. I also renovate my house regularly, working on different corners from year to year, making sure that I renovate—in effect, activate—the most auspicious corners for every year. This has given my home a life of its own so that it is forever young and surprising. My husband and I have lived in the same house now for 30 years and it is as filled with bright energy now as it was when it was first built. It has also grown considerably in size.

Feng shui is a dynamic phenomenon and, following this principle, I make sure that nothing in my own home ever stays exactly the same from year to year. As a result my home is regularly recharged with yang energy.

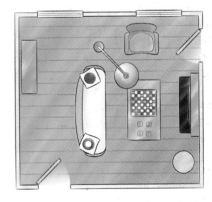

Rearrange furniture in living spaces regularly or, at the least, move it away from the walls and clean thoroughly. Here the table and sofa move opposite the fireplace and the chair and log basket swap positions.

65   Observe the renovation taboos every year

Regularly carrying out small projects in the auspicious parts of your home will bring great benefits. This is especially true if you live in a house with land attached, or if you live in the country. Every time you activate the lucky corners of your home you will be amazed at how fast unexpected good fortune will actualize for you. In 2011, for example, the lucky corner of all homes is the northwest corner. If you activate the energy of this corner with building work, or other improvements, you are sure to attract some kind of positive outcome. In 2012 the lucky part of the home is the west and in 2012 it is the northeast.

There are also taboo areas to leave well alone. Renovations or other disturbances in these areas will cause misfortune to befall those living in the house. Visit www.wofs.com to find out the taboo parts. For 2007 the taboo sectors, which must be left well alone, are the northeast and the west and, in 2008, the south.

Carrying out renovations, such as giving walls and ceiling a fresh coat of paint, in the auspicious sector of your home for the year brings good luck, but avoid working in taboo areas or your fortunes may change for the worse.

66   Bring in daily doses of sun energy

This is one of my most popular feng shui tips of all time as it is so easy to practise and brings so much happiness chi into the home. It is an especially effective way to make sure that the family stays together and that all members are blessed by the powerful rejuvenating energy of the sun.

Hang cut crystals of various shapes on windows that catch the rays of the sun directly—in the east during the morning hours and in the west during the afternoon. This breaks down the light of the sun, sending happy rainbow colors into the home. The colors of the rainbow bring in the cosmic power of newly minted energy. Remember that it is far more beneficial to tap morning sunshine energy than afternoon energy because morning energy is young yang, which stays powerful a lot longer to rejuvenate your home.

Always choose bright, sparkling cut crystals, not faded-looking ones. The more glittery a crystal, the more effective it will be at bringing new cosmic energy into your home.

Balancing the yin and yang of space

Sometimes the illness and misfortune that befall a home's inhabitants are due to unbalanced air that is caused by excessive dryness. When air is especially dry or polluted, the pervading chi of a living space becomes weak and overly yang. Spraying the air with water droplets is an excellent way for restoring balance in this situation.

The yin and yang balance of air in the home exerts tremendous influence on the prevailing mood of the household. It actually influences how residents feel. Scientists measuring air pollution have been astounded by the immense difference that polluted air makes to people's moods when they are exposed to it.

This is because, of all the examples of yin/yang imbalance in the atmosphere, probably the most serious is the imbalance that is caused by polluted air. Sometimes being exposed to certain yin energy-bearing winds can cause this imbalance. Examples of such winds are the Mistral winds of Europe, the Chinook winds of North America, and the typhoons that hit some of the countries bordering the South China Sea and the Pacific Ocean. When air is unbalanced, those who breathe it may suffer from migraines, tiredness, and fatigue. This is because, when air is unbalanced, the body reacts

Moistening the air by misting with water may help improve air quality and temperaments. Lavender (shown below) in its essential oil form can be added to the water to create a relaxing ambience.

negatively; it also has a negative effect on the way people act and interact with each other.

"Balancing" the air for better health

If you notice that members of your family tend to be irritable and short-tempered, succumbing frequently to allergies, headaches, and feeling depressed for no reason, you have every reason to suspect an imbalance in the air. Spray water into the air to soften it, thereby repairing this imbalance. Or turn on a fan to increase the flow of chi. Even if you do not feel the air is polluted or dirty, spray some water droplets into it. You will be surprised at how effective this can be in improving the tempers and attitudes of those in the home. This is because water also has a very calming effect. If you wish, you can add a few drops of lavender to it, or another scent that soothes you.

Chapter Two

Feng Shui Formulas
For a Happy Home

Alongside the physical elements of feng shui there is a second, equally important dimension of influence: time. The tips in the previous section will transform the spatial energy in your home, making the physical positive and auspicious while ensuring any feelings of stagnation and despair become a thing of the past. With these mastered, it is vital to make the best of time chi, learning how to update your feng shui in accordance with changing time periods, and also with the feng shui calendar from year to year.

Discovering how the Chinese lunar calendar can be expressed in term of the five elements and the 12 animals of the zodiac, how time exerts its influence through the Hsia calendar and its 20-year periods, how to incorporate the findings into your home with flying star charts, and how to optimize the energy of your home using your Kua number can all enhance the power of feng shui in your life.

Learn flying star feng shui

The fundamentals of flying star feng shui are the compass direction of your home, which gives its facing direction, and the associated flying star natal chart (shown below).

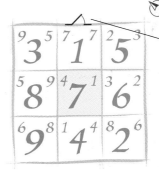

The door in the top center square indicates the facing direction of your home, so you can stand inside your main door pointing the chart toward it for easy orientation.

This compass formula method adds the extra dimensions of time and periods to the practice of feng shui. It enables you to identify the different types of intangible energies that constantly impact on the health and luck of physical structures—homes or other buildings. Learning flying star adds a new perspective to the practice of feng shui and, because it is technical in its approach, it is also easier to learn and to teach.

Using the charts
Flying star feng shui addresses chi energy by studying charts that are essentially based on the age of the building and its facing direction. The key is to identify the correct flying star chart that applies to the house you are analyzing. The method requires the analysis of the numbers in the nine sectors of that particular chart. By superimposing the correct flying star chart over your home—using compass directions as your markers—you can systematically study the quality and quantity of the luck of every sector and corner of your house. In this way, you can suppress any intangible bad energy and, likewise, enhance lucky good energy.

Flying star practice requires that you have a strong grounding in the fundamentals of feng shui; specifically, it requires an in-depth knowledge of the five elements—what they are, what they stand for, and their associated attributes. In the ancient texts on flying star feng shui, the five-element theory is always cited as the basis for remedies and recommended enhancers.

69 Understand numbers to practice flying star

Note that the "stars" of flying star feng shui refer to numbers, and the flying star system is not unlike the study of numerology as applied to feng shui. Single numbers have good and bad connotations, lucky and unlucky meanings. Combinations of the numbers have deeper implications of good and bad luck, good fortune and misfortune. And, depending on the number of each of the wealth or the relationship "stars", they reveal the potential for wealth and relationship luck. Numbers, however, have different strengths, different potencies, and even different meanings during different periods of time. To practice flying star effectively to a high level, you have to become familiar with the meanings assigned to numbers, and also be aware of their relative strength at different time periods. We are currently in period 8, which began on February 4, 2004 and will last until 2024—a period of 20 years. This is, therefore, an excellent time to add the dimension of "time" to your feng shui practice, since what is done in these early years of period 8 is likely to benefit you for the next two decades.

Meanings of numbers
The following meanings of flying star numbers are useful to bear in mind, as in order to identify the good and bad star numbers you need to know the meanings of the numbers from 1 to 9. Below is a simple summary, but for detailed information on each of the numbers and their meanings see Tip 79.

* Numbers 2, 3, 5, and 7 bring afflictions. Use remedies to counter their effect on the space they occupy in your home.

* The numbers 1, 4, 6, and 8 bring bonanzas and great good fortune. The luckiest number of the four is 8. Collectively, numbers 1, 6, and 8 are known as the white numbers, for wherever they occur they bring good fortune. The number 4 brings love and education luck.

*Number 9 is a magnifying number, enhancing the effect of good and bad numbers wherever it occurs.

Only the numbers on your home's flying star chart count in flying star feng shui—not your house number.

All three numbers in each square of this flying star chart are analyzed to determine if they are auspicious or afflicted. However, the smaller numbers exert a greater influence and so are more important than the big numbers in the center.

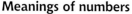

5	9 9	5 6
6	**2**	
6 8	4 1	2
5	**7**	
1	4 8	6 3
1	**3**	

Recognize flying star charts

Flying star charts apply to all buildings—houses, apartment blocks, offices, and other properties—that are built and completed, or massively renovated, within a 20-year period. Period 7 houses, for example, are those built or renovated between February 4, 1984 and February 4, 2004—the 20 years ruled by the number 7. Hence, these buildings are referred to as period 7 buildings. Houses that are, or will be, built or renovated between February 4, 2004 and February 4, 2024 are known as period 8 houses. Houses deemed to belong to the current period are always said to have much more vigorous energy than those that belong to the immediately preceding period, and so have a greater potential to be lucky and auspicious.

Every building has a facing direction, determined by the compass, that forms the basis of its flying star chart.

The 24 directions

There are altogether 16 charts that show the distribution of luck in 16 types of home. The categorization of homes is based upon the facing direction of the building. There are in total 24 possible directions, and these refer to the three sub-directions of all eight directions of the compass. Thus, there will be South 1, South 2, and South 3, and North 1, North 2, and North 3 directions. So, every main direction of 45° marked in the compass is divided into three sub-directions that comprise 15° of the compass.

The essence of compass feng shui

For the purposes of categorizing houses, the flying star formula recognizes two facing directions per compass direction. Thus for houses facing South there are two charts—one for houses facing South 1 and another for houses facing South 2 and 3 (see the Lo Pan compass in Tip 11). It is the same for all eight major directions. So, for each period there are 16 different charts based on 16 types of house. In every house, the distribution of luck energy is different—in one type of house, certain corners are auspicious and other parts are afflicted. Knowing this, the chi energy of the various rooms

of the house can be enhanced or corrected, as the case may be. This is the essence of compass feng shui, so the first step to using flying star to improve the feng shui of your house calls for you to familiarize yourself with the charts and the numbers indicated.

Q & A

Q: Why are there just two grids for three directions?

A: Because the grids for the second and third sub-directions are always exactly the same. For example, there is one grid for South 1 and another for South 2 and South 3 because the grids for these second and third sub-directions are the same. So the grids are expressed as South 1 and South 2/3.

71   Feng shui house charts

Flying star feng shui expresses the secrets of house luck in numbers. Thus, numbers from 1 to 9 are placed in a three-by-three square grid that is then overlaid on a building floorplan to mark out the luck of different sectors of any house, creating a chart of numbers known as a feng shui house chart. This method of feng shui has always been extremely popular in Hong Kong and Taiwan. In recent years it has enjoyed a major revival in China as the country opens up to embrace the traditional cultural influences of its past once again. In the world outside China, feng shui practitioners are also beginning to discover the magic of the numbers of the feng shui house chart.

The numbers in a flying star chart are each likened to "stars" that bring good or bad luck. By using flying stars to assess the luck of different parts of the home, we address changes of chi energy over time. We read the luck by studying the feng shui house charts.

Each specially constructed house charts reveals the secrets of energy within any building, with the luck of each sector expressed by numbers. There are numbers to denote wealth luck, relationship luck, health luck, and so forth while others also offer timely warnings of illness, afflictive situations, accidents, and misfortunes. There is therefore an element of forecasting that predicts possible misfortunes in this method of feng shui, so it is an extremely useful numerology aspect of feng shui practice that is extremely beneficial to learn and use to improve one's overall luck.

Let the sectors govern your home

Different numbers in each sector of the house chart will forecast different types of luck, so there are combinations of two or three numbers that reveal the quality of house luck. This method of feng shui also tracks the changes of energy over time as the Chinese have always believed in this concept. Everyone's luck changes with the passage of time and the challenge of feng shui is to keep track of the changes of energy so that we are then able to protect ourselves against times of bad luck, as well as enhance the energies surrounding us during periods of good fortune.

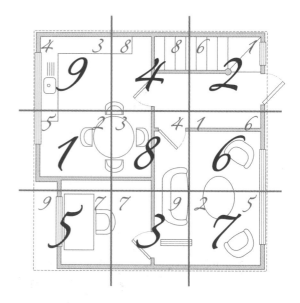

Each feng shui house chart, or "flying star" chart, is linked with the time a house was built or renovated and its facing direction. It reveals a home's luck expressed using the numbers 1 to 9.

How to read a typical flying star chart

72

This is what a typical flying star chart looks like. It is made up of nine grids that mirror the nine squares of the Lo Shu square (the ancient formula found on the back of a tortoise in Chinese mythology). Inside each grid are three numbers. The large number is the Period star and shows the Period number in each sector. In the center grid, the Period number is 7, so we know this is a Period 7 chart. On the right of the Period star in every grid is a smaller number representing the water star, and on the left is a number representing the mountain star. This arrangement of numbers occurs in every grid.

How numbers reveal luck

All three numbers tell you something about the luck of the part of the house they correspond to. Remember that in flying star feng shui the compass is always used (see Tip 11). So, to know the luck of the Northwest corner of your home, you have to use the compass to identify the Northwest, and in the chart being used as an example here, that will be the corner where the Period star is 8—a very lucky

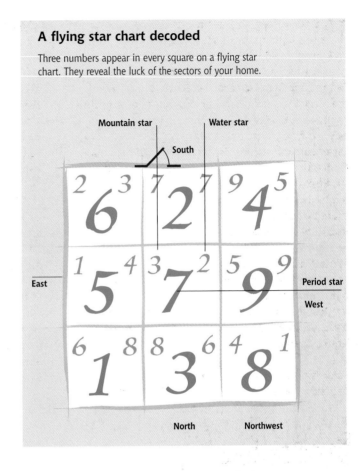

A flying star chart decoded

Three numbers appear in every square on a flying star chart. They reveal the luck of the sectors of your home.

Mountain star — Water star — South — East — Period star — West — North — Northwest

number. The water star is 1 and since 1 also represents water here, the water star is lucky. To activate its luck, place water (such as a pond, a pool, or an aquarium) here. The mountain star in the Northwest is 4, which stands for literary and scholastic success, and is also a lucky number. It can be activated with a crystal.

Activate the mountain star with natural quartz crystal.

73   Introducing water stars and mountain stars

Numbers indicate whether the water and mountain stars bring good luck or affliction. Water stars govern the luck of money, wealth, income, career, and material success. Mountain stars indicate relationship and health luck and generally specify whether or not a home has happy and joyous chi energy. In period 7, wealth accumulation governed the collective consciousness of the world and, thus, activating the auspicious water stars of the home tended to dominate. So making money and getting rich were the buzz words of period 7 because the ruling trigram, Tui, stands for the lake—water symbolizes money.

In period 8 it is the mountain stars that are far stronger, because in this period the ruling trigram, Ken, stands for mountain. Mountain stars suggest a time of preparation, when meditation, introspection, and a turning toward less materialistic pursuits become increasingly important. So, in period 8 you will find that there will be a heavier emphasis placed on relationships and the pursuit of inner wisdom. Identifying the lucky water and mountain stars in your home shows you exactly which sectors to activate with water and which to energize

with crystals in order to improve your feng shui. In fact, correctly energizing your auspicious water and mountain stars is such a powerful way to enjoy wealth and relationship luck that for this reason alone it is worth making the effort to accurately locate these auspicious stars.

The trigram Tui (top) stands for "lake". Ken (above) means "mountain."

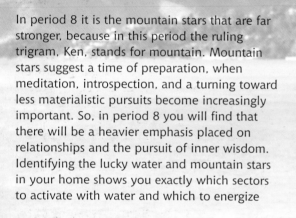

We are currently in the Period of 8

74

The flying Star method of feng shui recognizes cycles of time periods that last 20 years. Each of these periods is ruled by a number and characterized by the attributes associated with that number. We are currently in the Period of 8, a very lucky number associated with the image of the mountain, the trigram Ken, and the youngest son of the family.

At the start of the Period of 8 in 2004 (see Tip 72) came many changes in the energies of the world. Many countries experienced changes in leadership. Tastes, fads, and fashions also changed as did business models and ways of getting rich. In the years since the start of Period 8, the world has seen many and sudden changes and also experienced transformational paradigm shifts in the economic and psychological environments of the world. In fact the global village as a concept has become a reality as travel and communications have cut through centuries old barriers, fueled as much by technological breakthroughs as by new discoveries and inventions. The Internet and the computer have digitalized communications to such an extent that the world has shrunk and we must now look to the stars and outer space to see the bigger picture of our universe!

Period 8 is known as the "age of the mountain." The number 8 will be lucky until the year 2024.

beneficial to resonate along with it. Tap into it, using it to enhance your life because the number 8 is the key to unlocking the luck of this new period!

There are altogether nine periods of 20 years each, so the full cycle of feng shui time lasts 180 years. In each 20-year period, there is a reigning number and the ruling number of the current period is 8. In its own period, the ruling number reigns supreme and is extremely auspicious. So in the current period of 8, the number 8 becomes very strong and very vigorous. Utilize this number as much as you can to benefit from the energies of the current period!

The auspicious period
All this has happened in this particular Period of 8, an age of the mountain which reveals so much new knowledge to us. The world and all of us within it must adjust to a new kind of energy, the Period 8 energy. The number 8 has always been viewed as an auspicious number that promises wealth and success; but now it is also the number that signifies new knowledge and an ever-widening circle of connectivity that is sure to have repercussions. It is thus very

75 Period 7 flying star charts

The flying star charts of Period 7 are reproduced here to enable you to analyze the distribution of luck in your house, apartment, or office, if it was built or extensively renovated anytime from February 4, 1984 to February 3, 2004. Even though we have now entered period 8, if your house was built or extensively renovated in period 7, the charts of this period will apply to your home. It is likely that many houses will be period 7 houses. Remember to choose the chart that corresponds to your home's facing direction.

Using a compass

Use a compass to identify the chart that applies to your house. Remember, the directions move in a clockwise direction. When your house is facing exactly South or North, for example, then you know that it faces the South 2 or North 2 direction. If your house is facing slightly to the left of South 2, then it is said to be facing South 1; if slightly to the right of South 2, it is facing South 3. Note that as we move strongly into period 8, all structures deemed to be period 7 will lose energy. At the same time, the number 7, which was lucky during period 7, has now turned ugly and violent. So note the period 7 charts that have the double 7 in the front or the back of the house, for it is these houses that will get into trouble during this period of 8, making it necessary to implement changes to transform the building into a period 8 one.

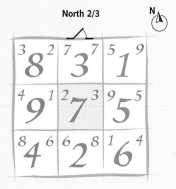

FENG SHUI FORMULAS FOR A HAPPY HOME

East 1 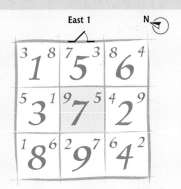 N

³ ⁸ **1**	⁷ ³ **5**	⁸ ⁴ **6**
⁵ ¹ **3**	⁹ ⁵ **7**	⁴ ⁹ **2**
¹ ⁶ **8**	² ⁷ **9**	⁶ ² **4**

South 1 — N

² ³ **6**	⁷ ⁷ **2**	⁹ ⁵ **4**
¹ ⁴ **5**	³ ² **7**	⁵ ⁹ **9**
⁶ ⁸ **1**	⁸ ⁶ **3**	⁴ ¹ **8**

West 1 — N

² ⁶ **4**	⁷ ² **9**	⁶ ¹ **8**
⁹ ⁴ **2**	⁵ ⁹ **7**	¹ ⁵ **3**
⁴ ⁸ **6**	³ ⁷ **5**	⁸ ³ **1**

East 2/3 — N

⁶ ² **1**	² ⁷ **5**	¹ ⁶ **6**
⁴ ⁹ **3**	⁹ ⁵ **7**	⁵ ¹ **2**
⁸ ⁴ **8**	⁷ ³ **9**	³ ⁸ **4**

South 2/3 — N

⁴ ¹ **6**	⁸ ⁶ **2**	⁶ ⁸ **4**
⁵ ⁹ **5**	³ ² **7**	¹ ⁴ **9**
⁹ ⁵ **1**	⁷ ⁷ **3**	² ³ **8**

West 2/3 — N

⁸ ³ **4**	³ ⁷ **9**	⁴ ⁸ **8**
¹ ⁵ **2**	⁵ ⁹ **7**	⁹ ⁴ **3**
⁶ ¹ **6**	⁷ ² **5**	² ⁶ **1**

Southeast 1 — N

¹ ⁸ **5**	⁹ ⁷ **6**	⁴ ² **2**
⁵ ³ **1**	⁸ ⁶ **7**	² ⁹ **4**
³ ¹ **3**	⁷ ⁵ **8**	⁶ ⁴ **9**

Southwest 1 — N

⁵ ⁹ **2**	⁷ ⁷ **4**	³ ² **9**
⁹ ⁵ **6**	¹ ⁴ **7**	² ³ **8**
⁸ ⁶ **5**	⁴ ¹ **1**	⁶ ⁸ **3**

Northwest 1 — N

⁴ ⁶ **9**	⁵ ⁷ **8**	¹ ³ **3**
⁹ ² **4**	⁶ ⁸ **7**	³ ⁵ **1**
² ⁴ **2**	⁷ ⁹ **6**	⁸ ¹ **5**

Southeast 2/3 — N

⁶ ⁴ **5**	⁷ ⁵ **6**	³ ¹ **2**
² ⁹ **1**	⁸⁺ ⁶⁺ **7**	⁵ ³ **4**
⁴ ² **3**	⁹ ⁷ **8**	¹ ⁹ **9**

Southwest 2/3 — N

⁶ ⁸ **2**	⁴ ¹ **4**	⁸ ⁶ **9**
² ³ **6**	¹ ⁴ **7**	⁹ ⁵ **8**
³ ² **5**	⁷ ⁷ **1**	⁵ ⁹ **3**

Northwest 2/3 — N

⁸ ¹ **9**	⁷ ⁹ **8**	² ⁴ **3**
³ ⁵ **4**	⁶ ⁸ **7**	⁹ ¹ **1**
¹ ³ **2**	⁵ ⁷ **6**	⁴ ⁶ **5**

76   Period 8 flying star charts

The flying star charts for period 8 houses are reproduced here (see right) to help those of you whose homes have only just been built or renovated (after February 4 2004). When houses are extensively renovated, it changes them into houses of the current period, and then you can use the current period's charts to give you an idea of the way the luck in your home is distributed. These period 8 charts are also useful for another reason—they enable you to make a comparison with period 7 houses to see which chart would serve you better, based on how the layout of your house fits into the respective luck maps.

Note that the lucky chi energy of homes built in period 8 tends to congregate around the middle of the vertical grids of the chart. This favors deep homes rather than shallow ones. As a rule of thumb, it is a good idea to have homes that are at least three rooms deep.

North 1

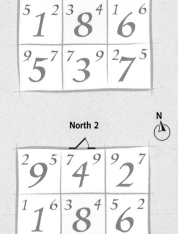

North 2

Northeast 1

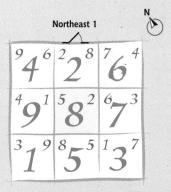

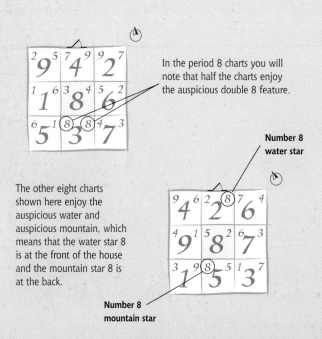

In the period 8 charts you will note that half the charts enjoy the auspicious double 8 feature.

The other eight charts shown here enjoy the auspicious water and auspicious mountain, which means that the water star 8 is at the front of the house and the mountain star 8 is at the back.

Number 8 water star

Number 8 mountain star

Northeast 2/3

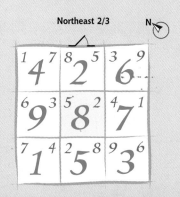

FENG SHUI FORMULAS FOR A HAPPY HOME

East 1
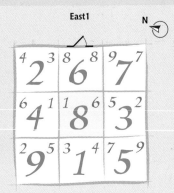

4 ³ 2	8 ⁸ 6	9 ⁷ 7
6 ¹ 4	1 ⁶ 8	5 ² 3
2 ⁵ 9	3 ⁴ 1	7 ⁹ 5

South 1

5 ² 7	9 ⁷ 3	7 ⁹ 5
6 ¹ 6	4 ³ 8	2 ⁵ 1
1 ⁶ 2	8 ⁸ 4	3 ⁴ 9

West 1

9 ⁷ 5	4 ³ 1	5 ² 9
2 ⁵ 3	6 ¹ 8	1 ⁶ 4
7 ⁹ 7	8 ⁸ 6	3 ⁴ 2

East 2

7 ⁹ 2	3 ⁴ 6	2 ⁵ 7
5 ² 4	1 ⁶ 8	6 ¹ 3
9 ⁷ 9	8 ⁸ 1	4 ³ 5

South 2

3 ⁴ 7	8 ⁸ 3	1 ⁶ 5
2 ⁵ 6	4 ³ 8	6 ¹ 1
7 ⁹ 2	9 ⁷ 4	5 ² 9

West 2/3

3 ⁴ 5	8 ⁸ 1	7 ⁹ 9
1 ⁶ 3	6 ¹ 8	2 ⁵ 4
5 ² 7	4 ³ 6	9 ⁷ 2

Southeast 1

7 ⁵ 6	8 ⁶ 7	4 ² 3
3 ¹ 2	9 ⁷ 8	6 ⁴ 5
5 ³ 4	1 ⁸ 9	2 ⁹ 1

Southwest 1

7 ¹ 3	5 ⁸ 5	9 ³ 1
3 ⁶ 7	2 ⁵ 8	1 ⁴ 9
4 ⁷ 6	8 ² 2	6 ⁹ 4

Northwest 1

9 ² 1	8 ¹ 9	3 ⁵ 4
4 ⁶ 5	7 ⁹ 8	1 ³ 2
2 ⁴ 3	6 ⁸ 7	5 ⁷ 6

Southeast 2/3

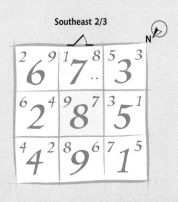

2 ⁹ 6	1 ⁸ 7	5 ³ 3
6 ⁴ 2	9 ⁷ 8	3 ¹ 5
4 ² 4	8 ⁶ 9	7 ⁵ 1

Southwest 2/3

6 ⁹ 3	8 ² 5	4 ⁷ 1
1 ⁴ 7	2 ⁵ 8	9 ⁶ 9
9 ³ 6	5 ⁸ 2	7 ¹ 4

Northwest 2/3

5 ⁷ 1	6 ⁸ 9	2 ⁴ 4
1 ³ 5	7 ⁹ 8	9 ⁴ 2
3 ⁵ 3	8 ¹ 7	6 ² 6

77   Identify the chart for your home

Each chart is based upon the facing direction of the house, so in order to identify the correct chart that applies to your home, first you will need to use a compass to determine its facing direction. Identifying the facing direction of a property can at times be challenging, since modular or irregular-shaped structures do not have a clear-cut facing direction. Besides, the facing direction of the main door is not always the same as the facing direction of the house itself. So you will need to make your judgment carefully (see Tip 78, opposite). The flying star chart also depends upon the age of your house—either when it was built, or when last extensively renovated.

Discovering your luck distribution

Before the recent surge in popularity of feng shui, flying star feng shui was out of reach of most people, and was accessible only to old-time feng shui practitioners. Here, I have made everything as easy as possible, so all you need do is correctly take the facing direction of your house and then see which one of the period 7 or 8 charts reproduced in this book applies to it (see Tips 75 and 76).

Next, use that chart to study the luck distribution of your home's layout. From there on, all you need do to make your home lucky is to apply the correct feng shui remedies to overcome the afflictions that cause misfortune, and enhance the chi that brings good fortune.

Project

Three ways to update your home

To get the maximum benefit from your feng shui practice, you need to research the natal chart of your home based on the flying star method (see Tips 70 and 72). However, you must first transform your residence into a period 8 home. To do this, you need to change three types of energy in your home:

1 Change the Heaven energy by changing at least some part of your home's roof or, if you live in an apartment, some part of its ceiling.

2 Change the Earth energy by changing some part of your flooring.

3 Change your own Mankind energy by changing the main door. Updating your home to a period 8 residence will be extremely beneficial because with the move into period 8 (which began on February 4, 2004) all houses can lose chi vitality unless these Heaven, Earth, and Mankind energies are revitalized. If you don't do this, you may discover that a great many afflictions start to build up in your residence—so it is best to update your property and enjoy the benefits of the new period of 8.

You can change your apartment to a period 8 building simply by painting your ceilings, which updates your Heaven energy.

Identify the facing direction of your home 78

To benefit from the compass formulas, it is necessary to determine the facing direction of the house from the 24 possibilities (see Tip 11) correctly and accurately.

The facing direction of your home is not necessarily the same as the direction which your main front door is facing. In most houses the main door and the obvious front of the house do face the same direction, but you should not assume that this is always the case. If they do face the same direction, then there is the potential for better feng shui. If they do not, then determining your facing direction requires some judgment on your part.

Making a decision
Take a good look at your house from all angles. Usually, its orientation is obvious to the eye and there are general guidelines to help you determine your home's facing direction. Having said this, there will be houses that present a challenge—modular or irregular houses, for example, are examples where some extra thought is likely to be required as there may be more than one outer wall which faces a strong source of yang energy.

For most buildings, however, look for the direction where there is the promise of maximum energy—for example, where there is movement, activity, and people. Or, the facing direction can be where the house window faces a pleasant view, a "bright hall" (an attractive space in front of the main door, such as a path or courtyard), or a valley. Only when you have successfully identified your home's facing direction should you use the compass to take that direction.

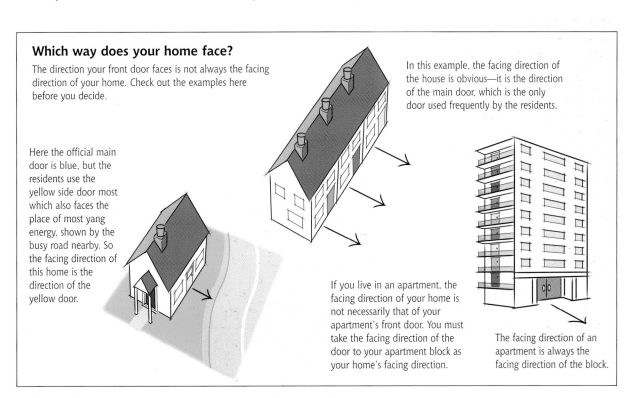

Which way does your home face?
The direction your front door faces is not always the facing direction of your home. Check out the examples here before you decide.

In this example, the facing direction of the house is obvious—it is the direction of the main door, which is the only door used frequently by the residents.

Here the official main door is blue, but the residents use the yellow side door most which also faces the place of most yang energy, shown by the busy road nearby. So the facing direction of this home is the direction of the yellow door.

If you live in an apartment, the facing direction of your home is not necessarily that of your apartment's front door. You must take the facing direction of the door to your apartment block as your home's facing direction.

The facing direction of an apartment is always the facing direction of the block.

79 De-code flying star numbers

In Flying Star feng shui, each of the numbers 1 to 9 appear on every flying star chart. All have a particular meaning, whether singly or in combination. Below is a summary of how their influence can affect your home:

• **Numbers 2 and 5:** Beware, as these two numbers stand for sickness and misfortune. Whenever they appear in any flying star chart, whether it is the chart of your house or the annual or month charts, take note that if you sleep, work, or eat in the sectors they appear in, you will suffer ill-health and misfortune.

• **Number 3** is the number of aggravation, quarrels, and hostility. This is the number that brings problems and misunderstandings. It also causes residents afflicted by it to have to cope with legal problems and unpleasant encounters with authorities. It must be kept under control, otherwise it will make your life hell if you become its victim.

The number 4 on a flying star chart represents learning and literary ambitions.

• **Number 4** is excellent for scholarship and literary ambitions. It is also considered to be the number for romance, bringing love and even marriage into a home when properly activated.

• **Number 9** is a magnifying number, making the bad numbers worse and the good numbers better. It is also regarded as the number indicating future prosperity.

• **Number 7** was very auspicious in the last Period, but period 7 ended on February 4 2004. Now this same number is associated with violence and burglary. Those whose homes enjoyed the double 7 in the last 20 years will discover that, now we are in period 8, it has become dangerous and must be countered.

• **Numbers 1, 6, and 8** are considered to be the "white" numbers and are excellent bringers of luck. Of the three, 8 reigns supreme, as this is period 8. The number 1 is lucky, but 6 is weak and does not have much strength unless aided by assistant numbers, such as 1 and 8. Together, this combination of numbers is believed to be hugely auspicious.

The numbers 1, 6, and 8 together are very auspicious—and identify a home's special luck sector. Here, for a North 1-facing home, the 1, 6, and 8 fall in the Northeast.

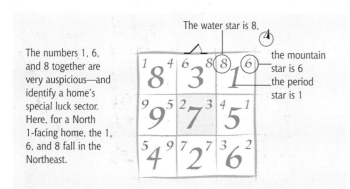

The water star is 8, the mountain star is 6, the period star is 1

Activating your lucky Water star for wealth luck

80

When you read a feng shui house chart, the intention is to activate the three most important types of luck that determine our quality of life. This means concentrating on our wealth, health, and relationship happiness luck. This can be done by looking at the Water stars for wealth luck and the Mountain stars for health and relationship luck.

To attract wealth and ensure that it remains in the home, lasting through into the next generation, you should look for lucky Water stars, represented by any of the four lucky numbers 1, 6, 8, and 9. Of these four numbers the Water star 8 is the most lucky and also the most powerful so look for the Water star 8 in the chart that applies to your home and then see in which sector it is located.

Wherever the Water star 8 is located you simply must have physical water in the form of a pond, a pool, or a water feature. The nicer the pool is the better and, of course, it should be yang, with movement, life, lights, or all three present. Pools by themselves may be lucky but they do little for your feng shui unless they are activated through usage and life which is one reason why the Chinese like to keep fish to activate good luck.

The Water star 8 gets energized and will attract wealth chi into the home when there is the presence of physical water, and usually the deeper the water the deeper the wealth luck! Thus the Water star 8 is best activated on landed property. If you live in an apartment, it is a good idea to invest in a good-looking water feature to decorate your living room… but only if it is located in the sector where the Water star 8 is.

In Period 8 charts, the Water star 8 is always located in either the home's front facing palace or back sitting palace. This is a very important observation about Period 8 houses and those looking to invest in a new house should really take note of this.

The facing palace is the front middle sector which houses the main door—hence its name. The sitting palace is at the back of the house and this is the center of the back sectors. For this reason I always advise my clients and students to ensure that the middle part of homes is kept clutter free and beautifully decorated with auspicious objects. This adds to the powerful effect of suitably placed water features.

Activate the Water star 8 for luck

The Water star 8 is a lucky star bringing good feng shui when it is in the front facing palace of the house. When the Water star 8 is at the back it is deemed to be reverse water! At the back the Water star 8 is said to be in reverse gear, and it is not as good as if the Water star 8 was at the front.

If you have an odd-shaped house so that the sector that houses the Water star 8 is "missing" you can still activate Water star 9 to energize future prosperity, or Water star 1 for business success. The skill is to locate the good luck Water stars in your home and activate those corners with physical water.

Water in your home or home environs activates the powerful Water star.

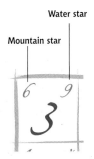

The Water stars sits on the right and the Mountain star on the left.

Water star

Mountain star

6　9

3

81 Activating your lucky Mountain star for good health and relationship luck

Activating the auspicious Water and Mountain star sectors of your house is one of the most powerful ways to activate good feng shui. While Water stars bring wealth luck Mountain stars bring good health and robust happy relationships into your life. Here the word relationship is used in its widest possible context and while the main relationship that a lucky Mountain star blesses is that of the husband and wife, a good Mountain star also benefits relationships between brothers and sisters.

Any home benefiting from a good Mountain star 8 that is properly energized by the presence of real or "pseudo" mountains is sure to enjoy a life free of aggravations and relationship problems—there will be little cause for misunderstandings to arise.

The lucky Mountain star 8 gets activated by the presence of mountain energy, which can be simulated by pictures of mountains, crystals, and walls made of bricks or concrete. The most auspicious way of benefiting from the lucky Mountain star is the presence of real mountains in the extended direction of the sector housing the auspicious Mountain star. Their presence brings amazingly powerful health and relationship luck.

Create your own mountain luck

If you live in a city then big buildings can also be viewed as mountains although, of course, natural mountains are always more powerful than man-made buildings either in a negative or positive way. If you live in an apartment, it is a good idea to invest in a good mountain painting where the Mountain star 8 resides. This is the best way of activating a good Mountain star.

As with the auspicious Water star 8 in all Period 8 charts, the lucky Mountain star 8 is also always located in either the front facing palace or the back sitting palace of the home. This is a very important observation about Period 8 houses and

Mountain stars occurring in the back of the home, boost relationship luck. In the house plan below, the Mountain star 8 is in the sitting palace at the back of the house, which is auspicious.

Auspiciously sited Mountain star 8

those looking to invest in a new house should really take note of this. The Mountain star 8 is thus either a lucky Mountain star or a reverse Mountain star. For good feng shui it is better for the Mountain star to be at the back sitting palace of the house where it is deemed to be lucky; when the Mountain star 8 is at the front it is deemed to be reverse mountain! When it is in front the mountain is said to "block" the luck of the house.

The sitting palace is at the back of the house in the center. If you can see mountains from here you will benefit greatly.

Misfortune luck numbers

82

When using feng shui charts always look at the three numbers in each square. All charts are read the same way using the meanings of the numbers to indicate whether they bring good or bad luck; just as there are lucky numbers that suggest good fortune, there are also unlucky numbers that bring different kinds of misfortune. Misfortune numbers cause a reversal of fortunes, bringing illness, accidents, business setbacks, quarrels, difficulties with the authorities... and many other problems.

Fight misfortune

The list of bad luck manifestations can be long and

the results are always aggravating, causing distress and sorrow for those who must endure them. People who have not experienced suffering

do not know what it is like and it is better never to have to go through sufferings of any kind; for these reasons it is beneficial to prevent bad luck from happening to you or your family or to at least reduce its impact. Loss and pain can be reduced to manageable proportions and this is what Feng Shui numerology, using the flying star method can do with great potency.

Unlucky numbers

The four unlucky numbers to be aware of in the feng shui chart are 2, 3, 7 and 5.

• Number 2 can bring illness or mental anguish; As with all annual stars it is important to know where it resides each year. In some years it will be weak but it can also be extremely dangerous

Year	Position	Strength
2011	South	very strong
2012	North	strong
2013	Southwest	very strong
2014	East	weak
2015	Southeast	weak
2016	Center	very strong

• Number 3 brings relationship problems; The number 3 is a Wood element number that is made stronger by the presence of Water. The position of the number 3 star in the next few years will be:

The rhino and wu lou counteract misfortune.

Year	Position	Strength
2011	North	extremely strong
2012	Southwest	aggressive
2013	East	very strong
2014	Southeast	very strong
2015	Center	aggressive
2016	Northwest	very weak

• Number 7 indicates robbery or loss of some kind: To guard against being robbed or burgled and protect your assets ensure that you counteract the number 7 star:

Year	Position	Strength
2011	Center	very dangerous
2012	Northwest	very strong
2013	West	very strong
2014	Northeast	strong
2015	South	very weak
2016	North	very weak

• Number 5 brings misfortune of all kinds. Also known as the wu wang it is the most dangerous star number of all. Suppress it every year with an all-metal bell or the five-element pagoda to prevent troublesome luck overpowering you.

Year	Position	Strength
2011	East	weak
2012	Southeast	weak
2013	Center	very strong
2014	Northwest	weak
2015	West	weak
2016	Northeast	strong

83   Being careful about bad numbers

Knowing about charts is one thing but you must also be alert to the dangers of the bad luck numbers, especially when they are hitting your main door or your master bedroom. If your house layout is designed in a way that means these two important sectors of your house are occupied by any of the misfortune numbers then you must put the remedies in place.

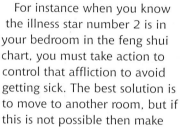

For instance when you know the illness star number 2 is in your bedroom in the feng shui chart, you must take action to control that affliction to avoid getting sick. The best solution is to move to another room, but if this is not possible then make

The pagoda

sure the room is painted white, the lights are kept dim, and there is a metal wu lou (this symbol overcomes the illness star 2) placed inside the room.

Door remedies

If the misfortune star number 5 flies into the sector where your main door is located, you can similarly take action to suppress the affliction. Here the five-element pagoda is the best remedy possible and it is really better to get a brand new one at the start of each year to ensure that its energy stays fresh form year to year.

In feng shui, the principle is to be protected against bad luck numbers at all times, but more so in the parts of the home you occupy the most. As long as bad energy numbers do not hit you, they will not be able to hurt you as badly even though the house itself will slowly lose good chi when troublesome afflictive numbers are not kept under control.

Dangerous combinations

There are three very dangerous combinations of numbers, the first of which is 2 and 3. By itself the number 2 stands for illness, either physical or mental, while 3 on its own stands for hostility and quarrels. However, when they occur together—for instance as the Mountain and Water stars in the same grid—the combination becomes an explosive indication suggesting misunderstanding or hostility of such severity that it can lead to fatal illness. If such a combination occurs in any year it is vital to place gold and Fire element as cures to subdue its power. This means placing yin Metal and yin Fire element energy: it is necessary for the yin aspect of the two curative elements to be used rather than the yang aspect as the yang forces disturb the 3, making it even more dangerous.

The second extremely negative combination is 2 and 5. Here, eiher the misfortune star 5 can combine with the annual illness star to bring major setbacks or the illness star 2 can combine with the annual misfortune star 5. The combination is so powerful because both are Earth numbers which allows them to give each other strength. If your main door or your bedroom has this combination I would advise you strongly to move out of the room temporarily or, if you cannot, place powerful Metal cures inside the room to exhaust both star numbers. Unless you are diligent about placing remedies to counter this combination the chances of you being hit by a major setback or a serious illness is quite real.

The third combination, of the 5 and 7, can bring robbery and violence though it is possible to feng shui one's house to be protected against burglary. Once you have determined that there may be some kind of burglary potential caused by this combination it is time to place your cures. The best is to place a blue rhino, or alternatively a blue elephant, near the entrance to your home. Water energy near the main door is also an excellent deterrent against burglars.

Locate the illness star 2 in your home

84

In flying star the number 2 is to be feared if you are old or suffering from a severe ailment, chronic or acute. When it appears as the water star 2, it suggests that your wealth luck is sick and your life is in need of some slowing down. If the mountain star is 2, it suggests double trouble, since it means that both the health and the relationships of residents living in that corner of your home, as well as in the whole building, will suffer.

Protecting your wellbeing

When the illness star 2 appears as a mountain or water star its impact is magnified, so you will need to take it very seriously. If good health is of concern to you, identify the flying star chart (be it period 7 or 8) that applies to your house and then circle the number 2 where it appears. This will immediately pinpoint the corners and sectors of your home suffering from this affliction.

In order to locate the afflicted sectors of your home, you will need to use a proper feng shui compass (see Tip 68). Consulting a floor plan of your home is extremely helpful for this exercise, since it is easier to find directions on a paper plan than by wandering from room to room with a compass. Once you have identified the place of the illness star, all you need do is suppress it with the correct symbols and elements.

The illness star 2 affects the energy of your home just as do an external feng shui afflictions, but the illness star's location is time-sensitive, moving around different sectors of the home over the course of a month, year, and 20-year period. The illness star 2 can disrupt the wellbeing of you and others who share your home.

Locating the illness star 2

Illness star 2 is a mountain star when it appears on the left and a water star when it appears on the right of the central, or period, number.

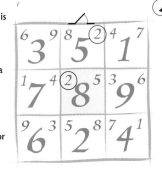

Q & A

Q: What if my house or apartment number includes the "bad" number 2?

A: This does not matter, because numbers are not analysed in the same way as the flying star method. So although 2 indicates negative outcomes in a flying star analysis, it does not indicate bad luck when it occurs as part of an address number for homes or office buildings. To know if your house number is lucky or unlucky, you need to use numerology methods.

85 Stay clear of the quarrelsome star 3

There is another affliction that can potentially be even more damaging than the illness star 2—this is the number 3 hostility star, also known as the bullfighting quarrelsome star affliction. When your bedroom or main front door is afflicted by the presence of the number 3, you will have problems related to misunderstandings, quarrels, anger, and hostility that can easily escalate. Number 3 is a Wood star, so when it occurs in the East or Southeast its effect becomes even more dangerous and fierce.

Water or mountain star

When the number 3 occurs as the water star, it suggests quarrels relating to financial affairs, and if it occurs as the mountain star it brings anger and quarrels into otherwise healthy, happy relationships. More divorces and separations are caused by the number 3 star than people realize, and I have often said that divorces are often caused by feng shui afflictions such as this. The number 3 star also appears in the annual as well as the monthly charts, and when they all occur together in the same grid, and if that grid happens to correspond to your bedroom, you will definitely be well advised to move out.

If the star number 3 falls in the sector of your bedroom, relationship problems can result.

86 Deal with the number 3 star

The best remedy for the number 3 star is fire energy, which means the color red and the triangular shape. So the most effective single cure is a three-dimensional triangular red crystal. This is a very powerful antidote to the number 3 star, and my advice has always been that if you do not know flying star feng shui you can place such a symbol on your office desk to ensure that, all through the year, you never succumb to the horrible effects of the number 3 star. Absolutely no harm will come from keeping this symbol near you at all times. The fire energy in something such as a small crystal will bring only positive energy. Placed on a brass or gold-colored base, the triangular crystal will become an even more powerful antidote against the number 3 star.

Other techniques

Alternative cures for the hostile 3 star include red curtains, red cushion covers, or a red painting hung on one of the walls of the afflicted room. Bear in mind that the reason for using red is the need for its fire energy to exhaust the hostile wood star. You can also use red glitter lamps to simulate yang fire chi.

Locate the deadly 5 yellow star in your house chart

87

In flying star feng shui, the most dangerous affliction is known as the 5 yellow. This is the number 5 star, and it brings a variety of misfortunes to wreak havoc on the peace and tranquility of any house, especially when the 5 yellow afflicts the sector where the main door is located. The 5 yellow is most powerful when in the South, as the fire energy here gives it added strength. Once you have identified the flying star chart that applies to your house—again based on its facing direction and also on whether it is a period 7 or period 8 house—look for where the number 5 appears.

The feng shui enemy

When the number 5 is the large period number in the chart, it does bring misfortune, although its effects are nowhere near as powerful as when the 5 occurs as a water or mountain star number—the smaller numbers to the right and left, respectively, of the period number. When the 5 yellow is the

If the number 5 on your flying star chart falls in the location of your bedroom, you will need to use a symbolic feng shui cure. The best cure for the 5 yellow is metal energy, which includes the sound of metal—so metal windchimes are ideal.

water star, it causes financial loss to residents living in the sector where it occurs, and when it is the mountain star it causes relationships to break apart and also the loss of loved ones. The 5 yellow is, therefore, the feng shui enemy of any house and should be kept firmly under control. It is also very powerful when it occurs in earth corners such as the Northwest, the Southwest, and the center.

Annual and monthly confluence

The 5 yellow also makes its appearance in the annual feng shui chart, as well as in the monthly charts, and when they occur together in the same compass sector, that sector is said to be strongly afflicted. If your main door or bedroom happens to be located in the part of the house where it occurs, it is likely residents will suffer some form of misfortune, loss, or accident unless the 5 yellow has been suppressed. Merely moving out of the afflicted part of the house is not really a solution, since bad energy has a way of leaking into other sectors. It is vital, therefore, to place cures against the 5 yellow.

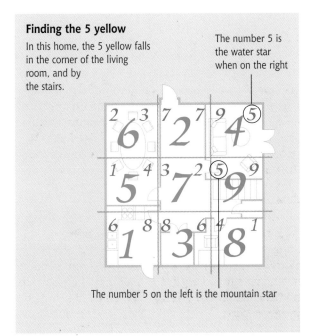

Finding the 5 yellow

In this home, the 5 yellow falls in the corner of the living room, and by the stairs.

The number 5 is the water star when on the right

The number 5 on the left is the mountain star

88 Take advantage of the auspicious numbers 1, 6 and 8

You should not get the impression that flying star charts have only negative numbers that bring afflictions. There are also positive numbers that bring good fortune, and foremost among these are what are often referred to as the "white numbers". These are the numbers 1, 6, and 8. These three numbers are said to bring excellent luck to residents of sectors corresponding to them.

The power of eight

Of the three white numbers, the most powerful good-fortune number is 8. This is because while it is already a lucky number (this being the Period of 8), it brings what the Taoists describe as the concept of double goodness, a double good-fortune effect. So when the number appears in the sector where the front door is located or even where there is any door, it brings in the good-fortune chi energy. For example, in the year 2005, the number 8 was

Look out for the number 8 when it is used decoratively, in patterns or even knots.

located in the South, so if your door is located in the South sector of your house you will have enjoyed great good fortune that year.

The number 6 is also a lucky number, signifying luck from heaven. But as this is period 8, the number 6 does not have much strength and it is not as strong as 8. The number 1, meanwhile, is also lucky, and in this period it stands for prosperity and good fortune in the distant future. The number 1 also stands for success, especially career success, and it brings good luck to your work. If the number 1 star occurs as the mountain star it signifies success in all your relationships; if it occurs as the water star, it means success in money-making matters.

The numbers 1, 6, and 8 are seen as particularly lucky in feng shui. You can incorporate these numbers in subtle ways in your home furnishings, as shown in this wall hanging.

The number 9 is the magnifying star

89

The number 9 is usually regarded as the magnifying star. Alone, 9 is a very auspicious number, symbolizing completion as well as the fullness of heaven and earth. In period 8 it is also regarded as the star of future prosperity. This is because it is the number immediately following the current period number, so it stands for the prosperity that will come after the current period of 8 is over, in about 20 years from now. In addition, we all want our prosperity and good fortune to last beyond this period, so the 9 is in this sense as important as the 8.

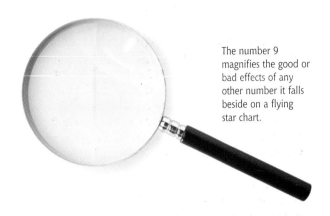

The number 9 magnifies the good or bad effects of any other number it falls beside on a flying star chart.

Good and bad

However, the 9 is also regarded as a magnifying number, so when it combines with good numbers (such as 1, 6, and 8) it enhances their good effects. When it combines with negative numbers, however (such as 2, 3, and 5), it likewise enhances their pernicious effects. So, whenever you see the 9 combined with the numbers 2, 3, or 5 in any flying star chart or annual and monthly charts, you know that it signals increased danger.

The number 4 is the romance star

90

The star number that stands for romantic luck is the 4, and it is best and strongest in its good effects when it comes as the mountain star. Then, all your love relationships will come to a fruitful and happy conclusion. Love relationships refer to the type that lead to marriage. When the romance star 4 occurs, however, all married couples must strive to ensure that there should not be any type of water feature placed in the sector of the home corresponding to that number. The presence of water will lead to unhappiness and scandals of a sexual nature. And then it is a case of romantic infidelities being discovered, usually leading to unhappiness and the break-up of otherwise good relationships.

Look out for the number 4 if you want to improve your existing relationships or find new romance.

The number 4 in an annual chart indicates peach blossom luck, which brings romantic liaisons and marriage opportunities. In the year 2011, for example, the number 4 is in the southwest of the annual chart; this means that 2011 is a year when females tend to fall in love more than males. The peach blossom in the SW is generally a good indication of family and marriage luck for the year.

91   Implications of period 7 coming to a end

The end of period 7 means that most houses in the world immediately lose energy. This is because it is likely that most of them would have been either built or renovated in the 20 years between February 4 1984 and February 4 2004, thereby making them period 7 houses. According to feng shui principles, however, as soon as the period changes, the energy of the preceding period's number loses vitality and strength. This means that period 7 houses need to be revitalized and re-energized as soon as possible so that we can welcome in the chi energy of the new period 8.

A change of luck
A second major implication is that the number 7, which was such a lucky number all through period 7, has now reverted to its original true nature, which is bad. The number 7 star brings burglary luck as well as violence and bloodshed. Not for no reason is it called the red star 7, and its element is metal. For 20 years this aspect of its nature was overshadowed by its good side. For 20 years the number 7 brought a great deal of luck to the many people living in period 7 houses. But the same people who benefited from the number 7 are now poised to suffer its bad side, unless they re-energize their house and transform it into a period 8 home.

92   The current period 8 and its influences

Inner values become more pertinent than external wealth and materialism as we feel the influence of the new period 8, which began on February 4, 2004.

With the change in period, the number 8 now becomes very lucky indeed. The number 8 is already a very lucky number by itself, and during the previous 20 years it signified "future prosperity." In its own period, the number 8 represents current prosperity, while the number 9 signifies future prosperity.

Changing fortunes
During the current period we will see attitudes transforming—for example, while 7 was a period that favored women, the number 8 favors young men, and its ruling trigram is the mountain, which stands for a time of preparation, or getting ready. The mountain also governs health luck and the luck of relationships. It is a time when the pursuit of knowledge is more important than the pursuit of wealth. In the coming 20 years there will be a refocusing toward family values and moral behavior.

Making money will become less important than the quality of lifestyle and having time to enjoy the family. Period 8 favors everyone whose Kua number is 8 (see Tip 106), and such people will find themselves very lucky indeed. And those living on the Northeast and Southwest axis—meaning those living in houses that face either the Southwest or the Northeast—will benefit hugely from the energies of the new period.

Changing your home into a period 8 home   93

If you decide to change the energy of your house or apartment into period 8 energy, some planning is required. There is bound to be digging, banging, and knocking involved, so the first thing you need to do is turn to the section on annual afflictions (see Tips 122–124) and note which corners are the auspicious sectors of your home (where renovation should begin and end) and which are the afflicted sectors that, ideally, should be left alone.

Take great care

When undertaking renovation work that involves disturbing the energy, it is crucial to avoid disturbing the places of the Grand Duke Jupiter, the 15° on the compass that corresponds to the animal sign of the year (see Tip 144), the three killings, and the deadly 5 yellow (see Tip 87)—these are the three places you really must not renovate, otherwise bad luck in the form of illnesses, accidents, and misfortunes is sure to materialize. Thus, changing your home to period 8 is not a simple exercise, but it is one worth undertaking if you wish to attract seriously good feng shui luck that will last until February 4, 2024.

Remember how to update

Here's a reminder of how to change the period of your home from 7 to 8:
• Change the building's heaven energy by changing the roof tiles.
• Change the building's earth energy by changing the floor, garden decking, or turf.
• Change the building's humankind energy by changing its main door.
In general, at least one-third of the roof, floor, or garden area will need to be retiled, replaced, or returfed. You can buy a new front door, but if you are on a budget, consider giving the old door a fresh coat of paint.

For people living in apartments, repaint your ceiling to change the heaven chi (see Tip 77).

When carrying out renovations, don't do noisy work in unlucky sectors—this disturbs energy and is thought to result in misfortune in the home.

Q & A

Q: What if I can't avoid renovating in unlucky sectors?
A: If you must renovate or carry out essential maintenance work, as long as you do not start or end your renovations in any sector that is afflicted, you should be fine. As long as you plan your renovations taking note of all the afflictions of the year, you will avoid activating misfortune stars and suffering their effects in your life.

94 Learning about annual and monthly charts

In addition to using the Period flying star chart of the house to feng shui your home, thereby ensuring it is not only a lucky house, but also a harmonious and peaceful one, it is also necessary to be aware of the annual and monthly flying star charts. These add the dimension of short-term updating to your home feng shui.

To do this requires you to follow the annual and monthly flying star charts. It is these charts that enable any practitioner systematically to update the feng shui of any house. Thus, every New Year it is incredibly beneficial to give your home a "sweep" of where the auspicious areas are located in that year, and also to where the afflictions of the year have flown. Take note that all the different afflictions of misfortunes, accidents, loss, ill health, quarrels, and so on are represented by the different numbers from 1 to 9, and it is by sorting through the numbers that fly to different corners of the house that a full and accurate analysis can be made. Only then can you update your cures and enhancers each year.

What are the annual and monthly charts?
The annual and monthly charts look just like the Period 7 or Period 8 charts, each with nine squares on a grid.

Shown here is the annual chart for 2011. You will see in this chart that the number in the middle is 7, which is referred to as the "Lo Shu number" of the year. In 2012, the number of the year will be 6. Note that in annual charts the center number follows a backward sequence. Only nine numbers are used, so after the number 9 appears in the middle, the year after that will be 1 again.

In addition, the annual chart also shows the place of the three killings as well as the place where the god of the year, known as the Grand Duke Jupiter, resides. To access the charts for 2012 and beyond, visit the extensive online feng shui resource center at www.wofs.com and you will see not only the annual chart updated, but also the monthly charts.

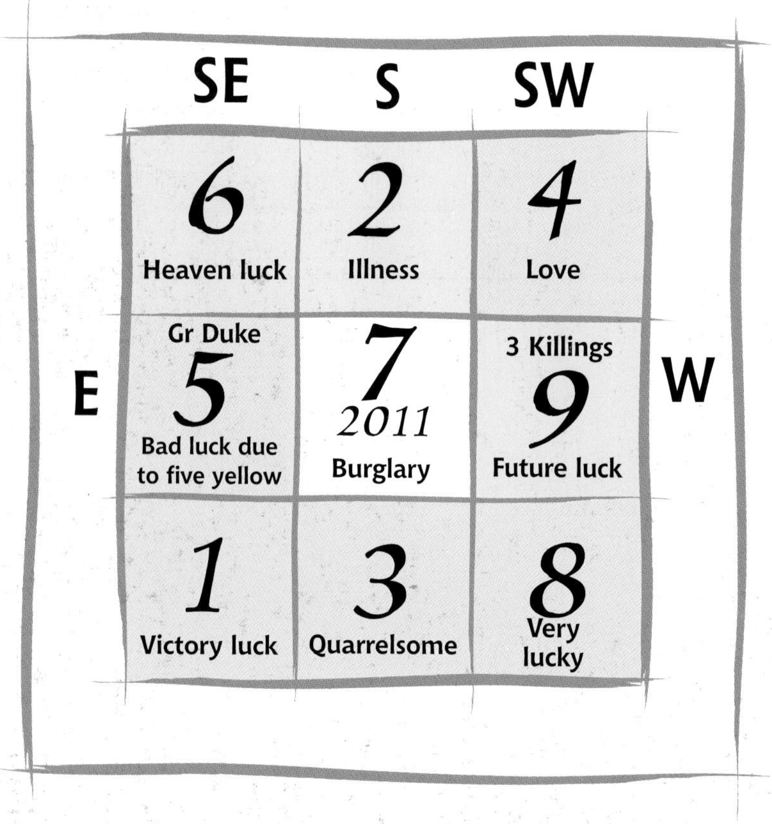
SE
S
SW
6
Heaven luck
2
Illness
4
Love
E
Gr Duke
5
Bad luck due to five yellow
7
2011
Burglary
3 Killings
9
Future luck
W
1
Victory luck
3
Quarrelsome
8
Very lucky

As shown in this 2011 chart, the Grand Duke Jupiter is in the East and the three killings is in the West. So in 2011 the East/West is quite dangerous and remedies are required for both direction sectors.

Auspicious mountain stars enhance relationship luck

95

For relationships to be positive, they need to be activated by the presence of crystal energy or fire energy, which in the element cycle produces earth. Crystals are the vast treasures of the earth, found deep under the ground and inside mountains. Crystals are the ultimate earth energy energizer, because contained within any rock crystal are millions of years of concentrated earth energy. That is why crystals will be such good and excellent feng shui over the next 20 years.

The numbers 1, 6, and 8 attract happy relationships.

Loving relationships

Use natural crystals to energize the auspicious mountain stars of homes and buildings. When placed inside homes in the sectors where the mountain star numbers are auspicious, such as 8, 6, 1, or 4, it will attract and create happy relationships. These relationships could be between man and wife, siblings, colleagues, or friends, as well as between fathers and sons, mothers and daughters, employers and their staff, and between lovers and sweethearts. The mountain star makes the relationships of your life come alive with love and support. It creates happiness, so if you want a happy environment, invest in good crystals and place them in the correct corners of your home. You can also use stones and boulders to activate auspicious mountain stars.

96 Use Chinese art paintings to activate mountain stars

If you prefer, you can use Chinese art paintings depicting mountains to simulate the presence of mountains in sectors or on walls that are affected by the auspicious mountain star 8, 6, or 1. These are the three numbers that signify that the mountain star is lucky.

Activating the sector in your home that is influenced by these mountain star numbers will bring you happiness and excellent relationships, ones in which you will make each other very happy. Just make certain that your mountain painting shows vast, soaring, friendly mountains that are colored with different shades of green. Barren-looking mountains are said to be more bad news than they are worth. So a verdant mountain scene that takes your breath away is the perfect type of painting. It is also better if there is no sign of a water feature in the painting.

When choosing art, opt for lush mountain scenes but avoid water, as this can negate the earth energy symbolized by mountains.

97 When good mountain stars are imprisoned, goodwill is locked up

Corners of the home that have auspicious mountain star numbers should, as far as possible, be kept open and free of clutter, so that chi energy can flow freely. This allows the goodwill chi emanating from the intangible mountain star energies to spread and flow to other corners of the home. Ideally, do not have a large closet or storeroom in the relevant corner, as effectively this keeps all the good luck locked up. If you have a large piece of furniture with locks in this corner, you should relocate it elsewhere in the home. Corners that feature good mountain stars are excellent places to position beds, sofas, and dining tables and chairs.

Different ways to activate mountain stars

98

There are numerous different ways to activate the auspicious mountain stars and the method you choose is entirely a matter of personal preference. Not everyone likes crystals, for example, and Chinese brush paintings of mountains are not exactly everyone's cup of tea. But the important thing to note is that unless you activate an auspicious mountain star as suggested, you will not enjoy the luck brought to that corner of your home. It does not matter how you activate the corner, but you must activate it to feel the full benefits of the auspicious mountain star.

Activating the mountain star

There are many ways to activate an auspicious mountain star (such as a mountain star that has the number 8, 6, or 1), but the best way is to create or simulate mountain earth energy. Therefore, try one of the following suggestions:

• Hang a painting of mountains.

• Build a brick wall.

• Create a pile of rocks.

• Display a collection of crystal.

• Construct a decorative room divider.

Hang a photograph or a painting of mountains to magnify auspicious earth energy.

Build a decorative rock pile to represent good mountain energy in the sectors of your home that feature auspicious mountain "stars" or numbers.

Construct and display a decorative room divider to create a structure with height, symbolizing the might of mountain energy in your home.

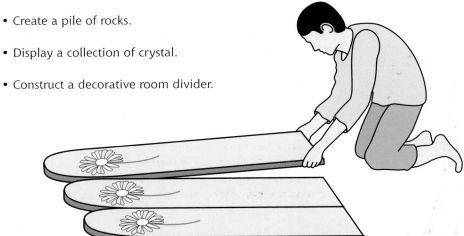

99   Lucky water stars bring enhanced income luck

Activating auspicious water stars for wealth luck is one of the most popular aspects of the flying star method of feng shui. It works every time, but to get this technique to enhance your prosperity luck, you will have to be very accurate in assessing the location of your auspicious water stars.

Always use a compass to detect your house facing direction, because it is only when you have ascertained the facing direction of your house correctly that you will be able to select the flying star chart that applies to it. After doing this, it is a matter of superimposing the relevant chart onto a plan of your house layout to orientate you in the correct direction (see Tips 75–78).

The auspicious water star worldwide

Finding the auspicious water star to activate is a method of feng shui that applies equally well to all the countries of the world—to those residing in the northern as well as in the southern hemispheres. There is no difference at all in the use of the directions and the charts. The flying star chart applies to your home in exactly the same way everywhere. Just remember not to estimate or guess at the compass direction. For accurate results, always take a compass reading.

Water numbers equal wealth potential on a flying star chart (see below).

Auspicious water stars are 1, 4, 6, 8, and 9.

Q & A

Q: Do the numbers of the flying star charts all apply equally in countries in the northern and southern hemispheres?

A: Very definitely so. Over the past ten years or so there has been a misconception in southern hemisphere countries such as Australia and South Africa that the application of compass formula feng shui required the directions to be flipped once you crossed the equator—in other words, South would refer to North and East would refer to West. As a result, those who followed this line of reasoning experienced negative effects from their feng shui practice. The charts and numbers apply and work in exactly the same way no matter where you are.

Exhausting the energy of bad water stars

100

When water star numbers are negative and bad, it is necessary to exhaust their chi. If you do not do this, they will cause you to lose money and suffer other financial loss. Negative water stars are those with numbers 5, 2, 7, and 3. If your luck is afflicted by these negative water stars, follow the advice below.

Countering money problems

• **The water star 5** is said to be afflicted by the malicious 5 yellow, which brings financial loss. To overcome the effect of the 5 yellow on your wealth luck, you should display plenty of large-sized metallic coins, as the presence of metal will exhaust the earth energy of the 5.

• **The water star 2** brings about financial worries and the stress brought on by money problems. To overcome these effects, use windchimes or six large, metallic coins. You can also overcome the water star 2 with an image of five bats around a longevity symbol—you can find this on a plaque or

Hanging a longevity symbol of bats protects against worry and financial problems caused by the water star 2. In this pendant, pairs of bats' wings are incorporated as a design motif.

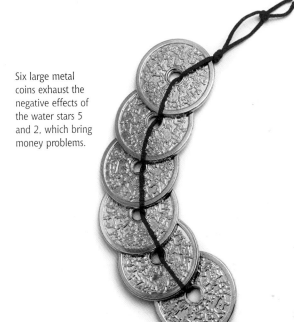

Six large metal coins exhaust the negative effects of the water stars 5 and 2, which bring money problems.

as a pendant (shown above). This will alleviate your financial worries.

• **The water star 7** either causes your money to be stolen, or it can bring people into your life who will cheat you. To prevent this from happening, you should install a small water feature in the sector of your home where the water star 7 appears.

• **The water star 3** causes you to have legal disputes concerning money matters. This is a very aggravating situation, one that is not at all pleasant, and to overcome the bad energy you should keep the corner afflicted by the water star 3 bright and well lit. Refrain from turning off the light, as fire energy will exhaust the wood energy of the water star 3.

101 Keep bad luck water stars locked up

One method of keeping the bad water stars under control is simply to lock them up. You can do this by locating a storeroom in the sector where the bad water star occurs. Often, however, it is not possible to alter the function of existing rooms or to change the layout of your home, but you can still take action—by placing a large cabinet in the afflicted sector. In the old days in China, special cabinets were designed exactly for this purpose. Once the negative water stars are locked up, their impact on the residents of the home is considerably diminished.

A cabinet located where bad water stars occur in your home locks up the back luck.

102 A six-level waterfall unifies the energies of heaven and earth

One of the best-kept secrets when it comes to building an artificial water feature is the six-level waterfall. This design of water feature is excellent for activating the double 8 in the flying star chart—this is where the mountain and water stars are both 8. The waterfall signifies the unity of heaven and earth, and when you place it near an opening into the house it also brings in the energy of the humankind. This coming together of the trinity of heaven, earth, and humankind is what excellent feng shui is about.

The six tiers for the water to cascade down are significant because the number 6 signifies heaven, while the downward-flowing energy signifies earth. In the broader landscape, water tumbles down the mountains bringing wealth and happiness to the people living below. If you wish, you can keep fish inside the collecting pond at the base of the waterfall. Otherwise, you might want to consider introducing plants and water lilies.

A six-level waterfall symbolizes the energy of heaven, earth, and mankind in harmony.

Your eight direction, or Kua Number

Each of us has a set of eight directions—four of which are auspicious and four are inauspicious—that is based on the eight direction numbers. The number that is assigned to each individual using this formula is known as a Kua Number and, based on these Kua Numbers, individual auspicious and inauspicious directions and locations can be identified and used to improve our personal feng shui. This is based on a potent formula that divides people into west and east groups with corresponding west or east group lucky and unlucky directions and locations.

I have discovered in over 30 years of feng shui practice that this personalized method is probably the easiest way to use compass feng shui because all you need to compute your Kua Number and find your auspicious and inauspicious directions are your date of birth and your gender. Once you know what your lucky and unlucky directions are all you need is a compass to help you orientate yourself to your lucky direction.

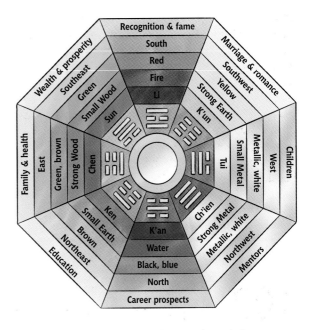

The eight-sided Pa Kua shows the element, color, and trigram associated with each of the eight directions.

Calculating your Kua Number:

Using your Chinese calendar year of birth by using February 4 as new year's day, determine your year of birth, adding the last two digits together. Keep adding the digits until you get a single digit number. Then:
For Men, deduct this number from 10. The result is your **Kua Number.**
For women, add this number to 5. The result is your **Kua Number.**
If you get two digits, keep adding until you reduce it to one digit—if you get the number 10 then $1+0=1$; and if you get the number 14 then $1+4=5$.

Example date of birth: March 6 1956
To determine the Kua Number:
$5+6=11$, then
$1+1=2$, then
for men: $10-2=8$ (deducted from 10)
for women: $2+5=7$ (added to five)

Example date of birth: January 3 1962
Because the date of birth is before the lunar new year, we need to deduct 1 from the year so instead of 1962, we will assume that the year of birth is 1961. Thus the Kua Number is $6+1=7$
For men $10-7=3$ (deducted from 10)
For women $7+5=9$ (added to five)

For those born after the year 2000, men will need to deduct from 9 instead of 10 and for girls you will need to add 6 instead of 5.

Once you know your Kua Number all you need to do is refer to the table of auspicious and inauspicious directions.

104 Four kinds of auspicious directions

The four directions deemed lucky for people from either the east or west groups can be further fine-tuned into four types of good-fortune directions so that there will be one direction that brings success, one that brings love and romance, one that brings good health, and one that brings personal growth and development. So, depending on what kind of good luck you need or want at any moment in time, you can use a compass to swivel your personal facing direction to capture the energy of the luck you want.

The four kinds of auspicious directions

1. Success—also known as your sheng chi. This direction brings success in competitions, and prosperity luck, as well as auspicious opportunities for growth and upward mobility. It is the direction to use in work or when doing business.

2. Love and Romance—also known as the Family and Marriage direction. In Chinese it is known as nien yen and also covers children and descendants luck. Sleep with your head pointing in this direction if you want to enhance your chances of getting married, of having a baby, of improving your love life, or generally improving the harmony of relationships within a family. It is also effective for making difficult children easier to control and more obedient.

3. Health and Longevity—also known as the doctor from heaven,

or tien yi in Chinese; this personalized direction is excellent for those who are older or are generally frail, either recovering from an illness or feeling weak. It is also a direction that protects one against premature death and is able to overcome illness chi brought by changing annual patterns of energy.

4. Personal Growth—also known as fu wei in Chinese. This direction benefits those who are still at school or in college as it is especially good at increasing your knowledge and wisdom. This is a direction that will be the most suitable for those taking examinations, doing their homework, and for those who are spiritually inclined for doing their meditations.

Discover your auspicious directions

It is a good idea to commit these lucky personalized directions to memory as this is one of the easiest ways to practice authentic compass formula feng shui and get results quickly. If you do nothing else save tap into your lucky directions, you will instantly enjoy excellent feng shui. Thus when orientating your sitting and sleeping directions, you must memorize what your personal success (sheng chi) direction is. Refer to the table below and memorize the specific direction that is good for you. Then try as far as possible to always sit directly facing the direction that brings you the kind of luck you want. Thus if wealth and success is what you want then go for the sheng chi direction; and if health is what is important for you, tap the tien yi or doctor from heaven direction and so on.

Your Kua Number AUSPICIOUS DIRECTIONS	1	2	3	4	5*	6	7	8	9
Your sheng chi (success direction)	SE	NE	S	N	NE SW	W	NW	SW	E
Your nien yen (romance direction)	S	NW	SE	E	NW W	SW	NE	W	N
Your tien yi (health direction)	E	W	N	S	W NW	NE	SW	NW	SE
Your fu wei (personal development direction)	N	SW	E	SE	SW NE	NW	W	NE	S
East or west group person?	E	W	E	E	W	W	W	W	E

* Kua Number 5, the top directions are for men, and those below are for women

Four levels of bad luck in directions 105

In the same way that you can fine tune your good luck directions, it is also possible to be very specific about the different effects of the four unlucky directions and these have an element of severity in the kinds of bad luck the direction brings to different people. You have already noted the auspicious directions, so to discover how the bad luck directions play out for you check the table below, Now let's take a look at the four types of bad luck direction in detail. They are:

The four kinds of inauspicious directions

1.   Bad Luck—also known as ho hai in Chinese. This brings mild bad luck that is more aggravating than severe. It is usually manifested by obstacles that delay your success, cause you to lose your cool, and are generally very annoying. But it is not serious so the bad luck brought is usually bearable. Nevertheless, these are the kind of things we can all do without!

2.   Five Ghosts—also known as wu kwei. This is more serious as it suggests that there are troublesome people in your life who make you miserable, unhappy, and stressed out! Usually the five ghosts refers to troublemakers in the office, people who politic against you and those who cause you problems by gossiping about you and spreading malicious, untrue or exaggerated stories about you. This kind of bad luck can transform into evil! It is a direction you really must avoid!

3.   Six Killings—also known as lui shar. This direction is even worse than the five ghosts as it involves six kinds of misfortune that stab at your heart causing you grief, heartbreak, and terrible sufferings. It usually refers to the loss of a loved one, money or assets, your good name, friendship, home, or the loss of good health. This too is a direction to avoid at all costs.

4.   Total Loss—also known as chueh ming. This is the ultimate bad luck direction, which can result in you losing everything that is dear to you, and necessary for your survival—perhaps through a natural disaster like a tsunami, or the financial meltdown of 2008. It is an extremely unlucky direction that should always be avoided.

Your Kua Number	1	2	3	4	5*	6	7	8	9
INAUSPICIOUS DIRECTIONS									
Your ho hai (Bad luck direction)	W	E	SW	NW	E S	SE	N	S	NE
Your wu kwei (five ghosts direction)	NE	SE	NW	SW	SE N	E	S	N	W
Your lui sha (six killings direction)	NW	S	NE	W	S E	N	SE	E	SW
Your chueh ming (total loss direction)	SW	N	W	NE	N SE	S	E	SE	NW

* Kua Number 5, the top directions are for men, and those below are for women

106 The eight-mansions Kua formula of feng shui

The eight-mansions method of feng shui categorizes houses according to whether they are East group or West group. East-group houses face North, South, East, or Southeast; West-group houses face West, Southwest, Northwest, and Northeast.

Finding your group

Those familiar with this method of feng shui know that it also classifies people according to whether they are East- or West-group people, and this is based on their Kua number. This number is determined by your gender and lunar year of birth (see Tip 103).

East or West group?

Once you have discovered your Kua number (see Tip 103) you can use it to find out which group you belong to:

Kua numbers	Group	Lucky directions
1, 3, 4, 9	East	North, South, East, Southeast
2, 5, 6, 7, 8	West	West, Northwest, Southwest, Northeast

Commit your Kua number to memory so you don't forget to capture your auspicious directions at all times. It will make a world of difference to your personalized feng shui. All that is required of you is always to remember to sit, chat, talk, negotiate, give a speech, eat, and sleep facing one of the four directions that corresponds to your personal (East or West) group. In the bedroom, as long as you sleep with your head pointed to one of your good directions, you are certain to enjoy good sleeping feng shui. So always take note of the East- and the West-group directions.

Always try to sit facing one of your lucky directions when you are working, eating, and even watching TV. For good family relationships, sleep with your head pointing toward your lucky nien yen direction (see Tip 19).

Using your lucky directions 107

If you use this eight-mansions method of eight directions feng shui, based on your Kua Number, you will find that, over time, life becomes a lot easier and more pleasant for you—good and auspicious feng shui is quite magical but when good luck happens it sort of creeps up on you. It does not occur in any dramatic fashion and it will only be as you look back over a month's practice or so that you come to realize that indeed life has become more pleasant, people are being nicer to you, opportunities are indeed opening up, and you are feeling more lucky.

To use your good-luck directions, it is a good idea to commit your four lucky directions to memory and then to always carry a pocket compass so that you never inadvertently end up facing a bad luck direction. We have seen just how bad these negative directions can be, so whenever you are involved in doing something relatively important such as facing a customer, your boss, your client,

Face your lucky directions according to your Kua Number.

or simply interacting with friends, then even just shifting your weight to face your good direction will make a difference!

At first you might find this odd, but after a week of practice it will become second nature for you. Remember to arrange all your sitting-room chairs and your bed to benefit every member of the family so that all are sitting and facing their good luck directions whenever possible.

Avoiding your unlucky directions 108

Always face an auspicious direction when at home.

While it is excellent to face an auspicious direction whenever you are engaged in a productive pursuit, it is even more important to ensure that you never ever have to face your personalized unlucky direction. This is something you should consciously avoid, especially once you are aware that there is indeed such a thing as a bad luck bringing direction.

You would not believe how many of my most successful consultations have been simply rearranging furniture at work for people so they sit facing an auspicious direction. Those who had suffered from facing their bad direction almost always saw a difference immediately. These were among my most satisfying moments as it was also easy to help them maintain their much improved feng shui. Teaching people to use this eight-mansions method of feng shui has always led them to wanting to learn more and it is usually only after using this method that they graduate on to learning flying star, another method which, of course, use numbers and directions of the compass.

109 The eight-mansions house luck map

The eight-mansions formula (see Tips 41 and 106) is not just a personalized formula—it also reveals the luck distribution in any home. Every building can be categorized as one of eight types of house, based on its facing direction. Usually this also means the facing direction of the main door, but if the main door is a side door, then generally it is the facing direction of the house gate or place of most yang energy.

Using the chart

The eight-mansions chart shows which sectors of the house enjoy the four types of good luck and the four types of bad luck (see right).

Based on your house facing direction, you can identify the eight-mansion chart that applies to your home. Select the correct chart and superimpose it on a floor plan to identify the good- and bad-luck sectors. The next eight Tips show you which chart applies to each of the eight facing directions, so all you need do is read the section that applies to you to discover how to improve each bad-luck sector. In this respect, note

The Eight Mansions luck map

Facing palace   Main door

NIEN YEN Romance	SHENG CHI Success	HO HAI Bad luck
FU WEI Personal growth	KUA 3 SITS NORTH	CHUEH MING Total loss
LIU SHA Six killings	TIEN YI Health	WU GWEI Five ghosts

Sitting palace

The four types of good luck are:

1 Sheng chi: prosperity, growth, expansion, success, and wealth.

2 Nien yen: marriage, relationships, romance, love, and family.

3 Tien yi: good health, wellness, and freedom from illness.

4 Fu wei: personal development and enhancement.

The four types of bad luck are:

1 Ho hai: mild bad luck, accidents, and similar events.

2 Wu gwei, which means five ghosts – people who wish to harm you.

3 Lui shar, which means six killings or six types of bad luck

4 Chueh ming: total loss and huge misfortune.

that it is always the facing palace and sitting palace, or areas, that exert the most influence on the luck of residents. Usually, the facing palace is front center and the sitting palace is back center, as shown.

If you work from home, it's important to check that your office falls in a lucky sector and, if not, use remedies to counteract any negative energy.

Optimizing the sectors in a South-facing house 110

A South-facing house is described as sitting North and facing South. Shown here is the eight-mansions chart of a house that faces South. Note that the sheng chi luck resides in the facing palace, or in the South sector of the house. Please note that sheng chi luck is regarded as belonging to the wood element, so wood flying into the South becomes exhausted by the fire energy of the South. Unless the wood energy of this part of the house is strengthened with the presence of water, the sheng chi luck that brings prosperity and success to residents will be curtailed. Thus, it is a good idea to place a water feature in the facing palace of this house. As for the other sectors, the analysis is as follows:

Wood in the South sector of a South-facing house brings luck, but it must be strengthened by the water element, such as an auspicious water feature.

Analyzing South-facing house luck

Romance luck, metal, flies into the Southeast, wood. Here, the romance star is strong, so there is no need to do anything here.

Personal growth luck, wood chi, flies into the East, also wood—so here wood is strengthened. There is no need to do anything, but do not have too much wood here as this causes over-competitiveness.

Six killings belongs to the water element, and when it flies into the Northeast, earth, it is pressed down by earth energy. There is no need to do anything as the six killings is therefore kept under control.

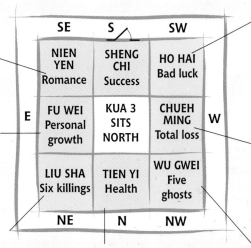

	SE	S	SW	
	NIEN YEN Romance	**SHENG CHI** Success	**HO HAI** Bad luck	
E	**FU WEI** Personal growth	**KUA 3** SITS NORTH	**CHUEH MING** Total loss	**W**
	LIU SHA Six killings	**TIEN YI** Health	**WU GWEI** Five ghosts	
	NE	N	NW	

Bad luck ho hai is earth chi, and by flying into the Southwest its bad luck chi is strengthened. So this house needs metal energy here to exhaust the bad luck.

Chueh ming, or total loss luck, is metal chi, and flying into the West, which is also metal, strengthens it. So water energy is needed here to exhaust the bad luck.

Wu gwei has fire energy, and by flying into the Northwest, metal, it is strengthened. Five ghosts' luck needs to be pressed down and exhausted, so place earth energy, such as crystals, in this sector.

The sitting palace (North) has good health luck. Here, earth chi flies into water so good health luck is distracted. Fire energy will strengthen earth and bring better health.

111 Making the most of a North-facing house

The North sector of a North-facing house—here, the front door sector—has natural good luck, which you can enhance with a water feature.

A North-facing house is described as sitting South and facing North. Shown here is the eight-mansions chart of a house that faces North.

Note that the sheng chi luck resides in the facing palace, or the North sector of the house. Since sheng chi luck belongs to the wood element, wood flying into the North sector becomes strengthened by the water energy of the North. So, the presence of water here expands the sheng chi luck, which brings prosperity and success to the residents of this house. So it is a good idea to place a water feature in the facing palace of this house, or do nothing at all as it is already lucky enough. As for the other sectors of the house, the analysis is as follows:

Analyzing North-facing house luck

Bad luck is earth chi which flies into the Northwest, metal. Here, the bad luck chi will be naturally exhausted, so there is no need to do anything.

Six killings chi belongs to the water element, and when it flies to the West sector, metal, it expands. Exhaust the water element by using lots of wood energy, so place plants here.

Five ghosts belongs to fire energy and by flying into the Southwest, earth, it is exhausted. There is no need to do anything further.

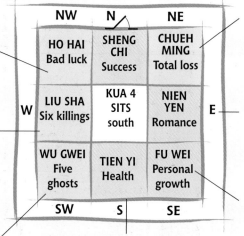

NW	N	NE
HO HAI **Bad luck**	SHENG CHI **Success**	CHUEH MING **Total loss**
LIU SHA **Six killings**	KUA 4 SITS south	NIEN YEN **Romance**
WU GWEI **Five ghosts**	TIEN YI **Health**	FU WEI **Personal growth**
SW	S	SE

Total loss luck is metal chi, and by flying into the Northeast, which is earth, it is considerably strengthened. So you need to use water energy to exhaust the bad luck here.

Romance luck metal flies into East, which is wood. Here the romance star nien yen, metal, is strong, so there is no need to do anything.

Personal growth luck, which is wood chi, flies into the Southeast, also wood. So here wood is strengthened and there is no need to do anything. Avoid too much wood here, however, or the energy becomes over-competitive.

The sitting palace (South) has good health luck. Here, tien yi earth chi flies into a fire element sector, so the good health of residents is enhanced. There is no need to do anything more.

Adjusting the energies of a West-facing house 112

A West-facing house is described as sitting East and facing West. Shown here is the eight-mansions chart of a house that faces West. Note once again that the sheng chi luck resides in the facing palace, or the West sector of the house. Since sheng chi luck belongs to the wood element, wood flying into the West sector is destroyed by the metal energy of the West. So, the presence of water here is vital as it expands the sheng chi luck, which brings prosperity and success while, at the same time, weakening and exhausting the metal that hurts the sheng chi. So placing water at the front of the house will greatly improve its prosperity luck. As for the other sectors, the analysis is as follows:

The element of success luck, sheng chi, is wood, but the metal element of the West sector of a West-facing house exhausts it, so display a water feature to strengthen wood.

Analyzing West-facing house luck

Personal growth luck, which is wood chi, flies into the Northwest, which is metal, destroying wood. Place water here to strengthen personal growth luck while exhausting the metal luck of the sector.

Romance luck metal flies to the Southwest, which is earth. Here, the romance star, metal, is strengthened by the earth energy of the sector so there is no need to do anything, except place love symbols to stimulate romance luck.

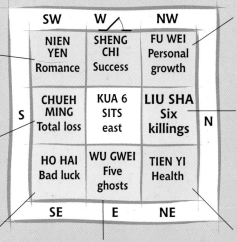

	SW	W	NW
	NIEN YEN Romance	SHENG CHI Success	FU WEI Personal growth
S	CHUEH MING Total loss	KUA 6 SITS east	LIU SHA Six killings	N
	HO HAI Bad luck	WU GWEI Five ghosts	TIEN YI Health
	SE	E	NE

Six killings chi has the water element and when it flies to the North water sector, it is expanded. Exhaust water with lots of wood energy, so place plants here.

Total loss luck, metal chi, is destroyed when it flies into the fire of the South. So you do not need to do anything here.

Bad luck ho hai is earth chi, and by flying into the Southeast, which is wood, it is destroyed by the wood chi. There is no need to do anything more.

The sitting palace (East) has five ghosts' luck and fire energy, enhanced by the sector's wood energy. Place earth here to exhaust the fire energy, such as boulders or crystals, and avoid a great deal of aggravation.

Good health luck has the earth element and is in the Northeast sector, which is also earth, so there is no need to do anything further. This home's residents will enjoy good health.

FENG SHUI FORMULAS FOR A HAPPY HOME

113 Creating balance and harmony in an East-facing house

An East-facing house is described as sitting West and facing East. Shown here is the eight-mansions chart of a house that faces East.

The sheng chi luck resides in the facing palace which is the East sector of this house. Since sheng chi luck belongs to the wood element, wood flying into the East sector is strengthened by the wood energy of the East. So the sheng chi luck, which brings prosperity and success to residents of this house, is enhanced. As for the other sectors, the analysis is as shown below.

The East sector of an East-facing house is lucky because it shares its wood element with sheng chi success luck.

Analyzing East-facing house luck

Bad luck ho hai is earth chi, and by flying into the Northeast, which is earth, it is strengthened. As a result it is a good idea to place metal element energizers here to exhaust the bad luck earth energy.

Romance luck metal flies into the North, which is water. Here the romance star, nien yen, metal, is exhausted by the water energy of the sector, so place additional earth elements here to strengthen the love and romance luck.

Total loss luck has metal chi and by flying into the Northwest, which is metal, it is strengthened. It is very important to place a water feature in this sector to exhaust the metal element and protect the patriarch of the family from total loss bad chi.

Tien yi luck, which brings good health and belongs to the earth element, is in the Southeast sector, which is wood. Here, earth is dominant and it is a good idea to include fire element energizers if you wish to improve the health luck of residents.

Personal growth luck, which is wood chi, is exhausted by the fire chi of the South. To strengthen wood and destroy fire energy, place water in this sector .

Six killings chi belongs to the water element, and when it flies to the Southwest, which is earth, the six killings' luck is destroyed. So it is not necessary to do anything more.

The sitting palace (West) has five ghosts' luck. Here, the five ghosts' fire energy is distracted by the metal energy of the sector, which it destroys. Introduce additional earth elements, such as crystals and boulders, to distract the five ghosts.

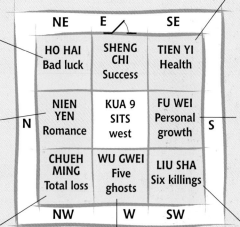

NE	E	SE
HO HAI Bad luck	**SHENG CHI** Success	**TIEN YI** Health
NIEN YEN Romance	**KUA 9** SITS west	**FU WEI** Personal growth
CHUEH MING Total loss	**WU GWEI** Five ghosts	**LIU SHA** Six killings
NW	W	SW

Capturing success sheng chi in a Southwest-facing house

A Southwest-facing house is described as sitting Northeast and facing Southwest. Shown here is the eight-mansions chart of a house that faces Southwest.

Note that the sheng chi luck resides in the facing palace, the Southwest sector of the house. Since sheng chi luck belongs to the wood element, wood flying into the Southwest sector destroys earth, the element there. It is a good idea to place water in this sector to strengthen the sheng chi luck. As for the other sectors, the analysis is as follows:

Analyzing Southwest-facing house luck

Romance luck metal flies into the West, which is metal. Here the romance star, nien yen, metal is strong, so there is no need to do anything for this sector.

Health luck, tien yi, which is earth chi, flies into the Northwest, which is metal. So here, earth is exhausted by metal. Strengthen the health luck with extra fire energy. Install a bright light in this sector to safeguard residents' health luck.

Bad luck has earth-element chi, which is strengthened in the fiery South. Install a remedy using metal energy to exhaust the earth chi of ho hai. Hang windchimes with six rods to dispel the bad luck.

Total loss luck is metal chi and by flying into the Southeast, which is wood, it becomes distracted. Exhaust the bad luck of chueh ming by placing water here.

S	SW	W
HO HAI Bad luck	**SHENG CHI** Success	**NIEN YEN** Romance
CHUEH MING Total loss	**KUA 5/8 SITS NE**	**TIEN YI** Health
LIU SHA Six killings	**FU WEI** Personal growth	**WU GWEI** Five ghosts

SE / NW / E NE N

Six killings chi, with its water element, flies to the East wood sector and is exhausted. There is no need to do anything here.

The sitting palace (Northeast) has personal growth luck. Here wood chi flies into an earth element sector. Further enhance wood with a small water feature.

Wu gwei, or five ghosts' luck, belongs to the fire element. Flying into the North it encounters water, which destroys its fire. There is no need to do anything further.

The element of the Southwest, earth, clashes with the wood element of sheng chi success luck. Water in the Southwest sector boosts wood chi and therefore success luck.

115 Pressing down the bad luck sectors in a Southeast-facing house

A Southeast-facing house is described as sitting Northwest and facing Southeast. Shown here is the eight-mansions chart of a house that faces Southeast.

In this house the sheng chi luck resides in the Southeast sector which is the facing palace. Since sheng chi luck belongs to the wood element, wood flying into the wood sector is strengthened, which brings prosperity and success to the residents of this house. It is a good idea to place a water feature in the facing palace of this house—or do nothing at all, as it is already lucky enough. As for the other sectors, the analysis is as shown below.

This Southeast-facing house has intrinsic luck, which is helpful for those living in town houses where there is little space at the front of the property for remedies and enhancers such as plants and water features.

Analyzing Southeast-facing house luck

Health luck chi belongs to the earth element and when it flies to the East wood sector it is destroyed by wood. Strengthen the earth element using lots of fire energy—install bright lights here for good health luck.

Five ghosts' luck belongs to fire energy and by flying to the Northeast, earth, it is exhausted. There is no need to do anything further.

Personal growth luck, which is wood chi, flies to the North, which is water. Here wood is strengthened and there is no need to do anything.

Romance luck metal flies to the South, which is fire. Here the romance star, which is metal, is being destroyed, so place earth energy, such as boulders or crystals, here.

Total loss luck is metal chi and by flying to the Southwest, which is earth, it is considerably strengthened. So bring in water energy to exhaust the bad luck of chueh ming.

Bad luck ho hai is earth chi and by flying into the West, metal, it is exhausted, which is a good thing. There is no need to do anything.

E	SE	S
TIEN YI Health	**SHENG CHI** Success	**NIEN YEN** Romance
WU GWEI Five ghosts	**KUA 1** SITS NW	**CHUEH MING** Total loss
FU WEI Personal growth	**LIU SHA** Six killings	**HO HAI** Bad luck
N	NW	W

NE ... SW

The sitting palace (Northwest) has six killings' luck, which belongs to the water element, and is flying into the metal sector. The six killings is strong and must be exhausted by wood, so place plants here.

Creating good fortune luck for a Northwest-facing house

116

A Northwest-facing house is described as sitting Southeast and facing Northwest. Shown here is the eight-mansions chart of a house that faces Northwest. Note that the sheng chi luck resides in the facing palace, the Northwest sector of the house. Since sheng chi luck belongs to the wood element, wood flying to the Northwest sector is destroyed by the metal of the Northwest. It is necessary to have water here to strengthen the sheng chi luck, which brings prosperity and success to the residents of this house. So placing a water feature in the facing palace is a good idea for this house. As for the other sectors, the analysis is as shown below.

A water feature such as a pool in the Northwest sector of a Northwest-facing house brings wealth to the residents.

Analysing Northwest-facing house luck

Ho hai bad luck belongs to the earth element and when it flies to the North sector it meets up with the water element. Exhaust the earth chi with metal energy.

Personal growth luck, which is wood chi, flies into the West, where it is destroyed by metal. Place water here to strengthen the fu wei luck while exhausting the sector's metal luck.

Tien yi luck, which brings good health and belongs to the earth element, is in the Southwest sector, also earth. There is no need to do anything, as the residents of this house will enjoy good health.

The five ghosts here is very strong as fire energy overcomes the metal chi of the Northwest. Placing water at the front of the house will reduce the bad effects of the five ghosts chi.

	W	NW	N	
	FU WEI Personal growth	**SHENG CHI** Success	**HO HAI** Bad luck	
SW	**TIEN YI** Health	**KUA 7** SITS SE	**NIEN YEN** Romance	**NE**
	WU GWEI Five ghosts	**LIU SHA** Six killings	**CHUEH MING** Total loss	
	S	SE	E	

Romance luck, nien yen, metal flies into Northeast, which is earth. Here, the romance star, nien yen, metal is strengthened by the earth energy of the sector, and so there is no need to do anything more except to place love symbols to stimulate romance luck.

Total loss luck is metal chi and by flying into the East, which is wood, it becomes distracted. Exhaust the chueh ming luck by placing a water feature here.

The sitting palace (Southeast) has the six killings' luck. Here the water energy of the six killings is exhausted by the wood energy of the Southeast sector. There is no need to do anything here.

117 Optimizing eight-mansion energies in a Northeast-facing house

A Northeast-facing house is described as sitting Southwest and facing Northeast. Shown here is the eight-mansions chart of a house that faces Northeast. Note that the sheng chi luck resides in the facing palace, the Northeast sector of the house. Since sheng chi luck belongs to the wood element, wood flying into the Northeast sector becomes distracted by the earth energy of the Northeast. It needs to be strengthened further and the presence of water here will expand the sheng chi luck. This brings prosperity and success to the residents of the house. It is a good idea to place a water feature in the facing palace of this house. As for the other sectors, the analysis is as follows:

If you cannot introduce a water feature to the Northeast sector of your Northeast-facing home, you can symbolize water by painting your front door blue.

Analysing Northeast-facing house luck

Total loss luck is metal chi and by flying into the North, which is water, it becomes considerably exhausted and weakened. There is no need to do anything more.

Bad luck ho hai is earth chi and is flying into the East, which is wood. Here, the bad luck chi is destroyed, which is a good thing, so there is no need to do anything.

Five ghosts' luck has fire energy and by flying into the Southeast, wood, it is enhanced. Place crystals here to protect residents from harmful people.

Romance luck metal flies into the Northwest, which is metal. Here the romance star, metal, is strong, so there is no need to do anything here.

Health luck, tien yi, which is wood chi, flies into the west, which is metal. So here wood is destroyed by the metal and needs to be strengthened, otherwise the health of the residents of the house will suffer. Place water here to feed the wood chi. Water also exhausts the harmful metal.

	N	NE	E	
	CHUEH MING **Total loss**	SHENG CHI **Success**	HO HAI **Bad luck**	
NW	NIEN YEN **Romance**	KUA 2 SITS SW	WU GWEI **Five ghosts**	SE
	TIEN YI **Health**	FU WEI **Personal growth**	LIU SHA **Six killings**	
	W	SW	S	

The sitting palace (Southwest) has personal growth luck, whose element is wood. Here wood chi flies into an earth element sector, so the self-development luck of residents still needs strengthening. Place water here to do this.

Six killings chi belongs to the water element, and when it flies to the South fire sector it still needs to be overcome. Exhaust the water element using lots of wood energy, so place plants here.

The powerful influences of flying star specials 118

One of the most exciting aspects of flying star feng shui is the depth of its many indicators of potentially powerful feng shui. Long ago, flying star methods were a closely guarded secret and feng shui masters of the old school would simply leave their clients bewildered by the array of recommendations offered. Seldom were explanations given, with the result that many people were left guessing as to the true reason for changing their door directions, tilting their entrances, or changing the color of their walls. All that was offered were dire warnings of misfortune unless their advice was heeded to the letter. Rare indeed was the 20th-century feng shui master who was patient enough to explain. This is even assuming that he was completely familiar with the esoteric underpinnings of the compass formulas. Most had studied under other masters on an ad hoc basis; few ever attended schools or went through the disciplined scholastic training we are familiar with today.

Modern feng shui

Those who study feng shui today from experienced masters learn best when their knowledge is supplemented by books, through carrying out research, and by practical testing. It is now excitingly possible for almost anyone to have access to the flying star feng shui methods of analyzing and advising on feng shui. If you wish to go deeper into the method, however, it is a good idea to know about the "specials", which refer to the different combinations of numbers that bring extra powerful good fortune. Houses that are converted into period 8 houses will be able to benefit from some amazingly exceptional luck. Listed over the following eight tips are some of the specials. You can either look for a house that demonstrates some of the combinations described, or try to transform your existing house to enjoy the benefits.

Flying star special formulas are based around the energies of the natural world—water and earth, or mountains.

119 Take advantage of the double-8 mountain and water stars

All houses facing the cardinal directions of North, South, East, and West will enjoy the double 8 phenomenon—this means that both the water and mountain stars (the small numbers to the left and right of a period number) are 8. This double 8 occurrence is located either in front or at the back of the house, depending on its facing direction. All houses facing North 1, South 2/3, East 1, and West 1 will experience the double 8 phenomenon in the front of the house in the center palace. These houses will benefit enormously from having a waterfall in front directly facing the front door to activate the

North, South, East, or West-facing homes' lucky sector is indicated by the location of the double 8s.

double 8 mountain and water stars. Bear in mind that the waterfall signifies the energies of both the mountain and water. Let the flow of the waterfall be gentle and design the feature to have six levels of water flowing down. Do not build a waterfall that is too large—it must always be in balance with the size of your front door and house.

120 Activate the period's direct spirit of the northeast with a mountain

Another important special, which is easy for anyone to activate, is to take note of period 8's direct and indirect spirit—these bring up-to-date strong chi energy. Activate the direct spirit, which is located in the Northeast of the home, with mountain symbolism.

The benefits of a mountain
This mountain can be represented by a little mound of stones, boulders, or a real heap of earth. If you live in an apartment, use a crystal geode to simulate the mountain—place it in the Northeast of your home to activate the direct spirit of the period and watch it bring you amazing support luck from all quarters.

You can also place a picture or painting of a real mountain range such as the Himalayas on the Northeast wall of your home. This will benefit everyone in your home, but especially the young sons of the family. Doing so will bring you much added income and wealth luck.

Mountain imagery benefits the whole family, especially the sons.

Display crystals to symbolize the good energy of mountains.

Energize the period's indirect spirit of the southwest with water

You can also activate period 8's indirect spirit by placing water in the Southwest. This is the location of the indirect spirit and placing water here will activate wealth luck for the mother figure of the home. Place a yang water feature here—it can be a pond, a pool, a waterfall, or anything at all that suggests clean, moving water.

The benefits of water

All through period 8, the Southwest corner of your house benefits from the presence of physical water—it does not matter what direction your house faces. This is where water can bring great good fortune. Moreover, if your home is Southwest facing, the Southwest sector is also visited by the very auspicious water star 8 (see the flying star chart in Tip 76).

I always alert everyone to the fantastic potential of all Southwest 1-facing houses. Even if your are an East-group person, if you can, try to find a house that has a Southwest 1-facing orientation and then activate the front of the house by displaying a water feature there.

When there is a small pool or pond in the Southwest of your property (preferably in the garden) it activates the indirect spirit of period 8, and this brings wealth luck. It also benefits the matriarch in particular.

122 Keeping track of changes in annual and monthly chi energy

This aspect of feng shui practice is a further development of flying star feng shui and is still not fully understood by many practitioners. It is part of the flying star system, but the annual and monthly charts that reveal the constantly changing locations of affliction star numbers and auspicious star numbers are different from the flying star charts of houses. The annual and monthly charts must be read in conjunction with the charts of houses. So basically what we end up with is a combination of five numbers in each compass location—these numbers give us a pretty accurate picture of what the luck of houses looks like from month to month and from year to year. To recap, these numbers comprise:

1 The period number (in the house chart).

2 The water star number (in the house chart).

3 The mountain star number (in the house chart).

4 The annual star number (in the year chart).

5 The monthly star number (in the month chart).

You are already familiar with the house charts of both period 7 and period 8 (see Tips 37 and 38), so what you now need is to become familiar with how to obtain the year charts and the month charts to give you an up-to-date picture of how the chi energy is changing in your house. The meanings of the numbers do not change, so the affliction numbers remain 2, 5, 3, and 7, each with its individual type of misfortune. Likewise, the auspicious numbers are still 8, 9, 1, 6, and 4, each bringing its own type of good fortune.

123 Feng shui updates for each new year

At the start of each new year based on the Chinese Hsia calendar, which always begins on February 4 of each year, it is important to assess the new year chart and the monthly charts to familiarize yourself with the new energy of that year. Here, we follow the Hsia calendar months, which are different from lunar months and the months of the Western calendar. The Hsia calendar is equivalent to the solar calendar the Chinese use to calculate the beginning of spring, and when to plant and when to harvest. It is the calendar on which many of the oracles and destiny methods contained in the Chinese Almanac, or Tong Sing (see left) are based. Once you understand the importance of these charts you will be able to use them to update the feng shui of your home. Bear in mind that it is the year and month afflictions that bring you the aggravations of daily living (see the sample chart opposite in Tip 124) such as feeling exhausted, quarrelling with people for no apparent reason, suddenly falling ill, getting robbed, being hit with an unexpected disaster, and just about everything going wrong. When this happens you can suspect it is the year and month stars playing havoc with your life, especially if you know that the rest of your space feng shui is fine.

The Chinese almanac, or Tong Sing, bases its predictions on the Hsia calender.

Be alert to dangerous star afflictions each year and every month

124

You must be absolutely alert to the dangerous star number afflictions that show up in the year and month charts. What are you looking for? Basically, you want to look out for:

- The misfortune star 5
- The illness star 2
- The quarrelsome star 3
- The violent star 7

Look at which compass sector they are located at in the year chart.

Forewarned is forearmed

Having found the location of these troublesome star numbers, see which part of your house is affected. If, for example, it is your facing palace (the part of your house that is in front and that probably has the main door) then you need to be extra careful. This is because everyone passes through that part of the house and if it is afflicted by the number 2 star, residents are sure to fall ill. Worse, if the month 2 is also there and if the mountain or water star is also a 2, then the accumulation of 2s will bring powerful misfortune energy to the residents.

Always identify any troublesome stars that afflict your main door, as this affects the luck of the whole house, rather than just the area around the main entrance itself.

SE	S	SW
6 Heaven luck	**2** Illness	**4** Love
Gr Duke **5** Bad luck due to five yellow	**7** 2011 Burglary	3 Killings **9** Future luck
1 Victory luck	**3** Quarrelsome	**8** Very lucky

E ... W

Shown here is the annual chart for 2011, the year of the metal Rabbit. It shows the lucky and the afflicted directions of the year 2011 – so note that the dreaded five yellow is in the East which is the location of the Rabbit itself. This is thus a highly afflicted year for the Rabbit. The center star 7 is also not a good indication as this suggests that the dominant energy of the year will be that of betrayal of trust. Check also the placement of unlucky month numbers as bad luck can intensify when bad luck numbers occur as both annual and monthly stars in the same direction sector. For updated charts annual and monthly go to www.wofs.com.

Then it will definitely be necessary to put cures into place or, better still, residents should consider taking a vacation during the month when the 2s congregate like this. This same outcome will also occur when the 2s congregate in the dining room area or in the bedroom.

If the year 2 is joined by the month 3, then illness leads to quarrels and severe consequences. The important part of the investigation is to determine if the bad star numbers affect any of the important parts of your house. Needless to say, if the affliction numbers fall inside a kitchen, storeroom, or toilet, you have no cause for worry.

125 Incorporating the Kua formula into your life

The Lo Shu compass gives the principle feng shui formulas.

Since the Kua formula is personal to you, it should be incorporated into your lifestyle so that you always use your best directions when working, sleeping, or relaxing. All that is needed is for you to learn your own set of good-luck and bad-luck directions and to carry a small compass around so that you are never caught in a situation where you have to sit facing a total-loss direction.

Eight mansions is so easy to practice because it is exclusively about orientations: all that is required is for you to tap into your auspicious directions. It

goes to the heart of feng shui because it uses orientations to ensure that you are always blending into the chi energy of your space.

Find and face your good direction
In instances when it is not possible to sit or sleep in the desired direction, you should try to use one of your other three good directions. It may not be the direction you want but it is infinitely better to sit facing an acceptable direction than one that is inauspicious and spells total loss for you!

The formula describes the specific types of good and bad luck of all the eight directions of the compass but whenever you are unable to tap the direction that you want then it is a good idea to be creative about your feng shui arrangement of furniture. In the practice of feng shui, you will find that on a practical level you always need to decide on the trade offs involved—perhaps giving up something in order to achieve some particular feng shui arrangement. When it comes to sleeping and facing directions at home, however, if there is a choice between getting hit by poison arrows or successfully tapping your direction then it is better to be protected from the poison arrow first!

126 What your Kua Number says about you

Your Kua Number also tells you your personal Kua element, and your personal trigram for feng shui purposes. This is summarized for all the nine numbers in the table here, showing all the information you need about elements and your directions for personal growth. These will help you to "feng shui" your personal space, to custom design color schemes, as well as the shapes and directions that benefit you personally according to your Kua Number.

Kua Number	Your Kua element	Your Kua trigram	Best color for your home	Best direction for personal growth
1	Water	Kan	White	North
2	Earth	Kun	Red/yellow	Southwest
3	Wood	Chen	Blue/green	East
4	Wood	Sun	Blue/green	Southeast
5	Earth	Kun/ken	Red/yellow	SW/NE
6	Metal	Chien	Yellow/white	Northwest
7	Metal	Tui	Yellow/white	West
8	Earth	Ken	Red/yellow	Northeast
9	Fire	Li	Green/red	South

Lucky things for Kua 1 people

127

In eight mansions feng shui, your Kua Number is considered your lucky number. Use a Kua Number of 1 to activate good fortune and success in your living space. Examples of this include selecting the 1st day of each month to undertake important projects, to have numbers end with the number 1, and even have the number printed on your T-shirt!

This is particularly suitable for people who live alone and for the feng shui of small office spaces. So if your Kua Number is 1, then you know that water is your personal element and that having a water feature is sure to benefit you. Likewise locating yourself in the north sector of a room or office is certain to bring benefits. And if you sit facing north it will be very beneficial for you in that this is the direction that brings personal growth, making you happy and energized.

Stay bright and white
The best color for you is white, as this is the color that has the best natural affinity for you. Wearing white will bring you the luck of authority and cause others to view you with greater respect. Those in managerial situations would definitely benefit from wearing white. Metallic colors such as

Kua 1 people benefit from white, airy spaces.

Auspicious factors for Kua 1

Element	Water
Color	White
Direction	North

gold and silver are also excellent for you, as are dark blue and black—the colors of water—so wearing both black and white benefits you.

Surrounding yourself with metal windchimes and bells placed in the north corners of your living or work space will strengthen and empower you. People who belong to Kua 1 always benefit from wearing white gold jewelry, especially those set with blue stones such as sapphires and aquamarines.

Unlucky things for Kua 1 people

128

With Number 1 as your Kua Number, however, you must also be aware of the taboos that can bring negative consequences to your space. Thus you must always ensure that the north sector of your home or office is kept especially uncluttered. Here the best color for the walls is to be painted white and the colors to avoid under all circumstances are shades of green, as well as all types of cream and yellow.

Reduce the amount of plants that suggest an excess of Wood element here as they will cause

your Kua sector in the north to become exhausted. Instead place more metal objects or furniture in the north.

Those with Kua Number 1 should also reduce the amount of green they wear, as the Wood element energy this represents does nothing for you. Yellow or earth colors are also not good colors for you. You should avoid wearing crystals, and yellow and green stones—so don't wear emeralds, green tourmalines, and citrines as these could well bring mishaps and obstacles into your life.

129 Lucky things for Kua 2 people

Knowing all the things that bring you luck is sure to help you to feng shui your personal space more effectively and accurately. One of the best ways of doing this is to use your personal Kua Number as a guide to all that is good and bad for you personally as well as for your space.

If your Kua Number is 2, Earth energy is superb for you, as Big Earth is your personal element, so having some kind of mountain-type feature nearby is sure to benefit you. This can be a painting hanging behind you, or the presence of a globe, perhaps made of crystal or some kind of ceramic material. The presence of the Earth element will instantly strengthen your environmental feng shui, and if you have these enhancers in a pair it is even better because it emphasizes the number 2 that is so lucky for you.

Enhance the southwest
Likewise, locating yourself in the southwest sector of your room, or the southwest corner of the office is certain to bring benefits for you as this is the direction that brings personal growth, making you effective and very productive. It will also attract powerful women into your life who have

the inclination to help you! To make the southwest even more powerful place a bright red lamp here.

Your best colors are earth tones from yellow to gold and red is also suitable—wearing earthy colors if you are also well tanned will also make the Earth Goddess of the southwest very auspicious. The gemstones that suit you best are golden topazes, citrines, and all red stones such as rubies. Crystals are also excellent as these activate the Earth energies of the cosmic universe very efficiently. Wearing crystals, and better yet diamonds, will enhance your personal feng shui enormously.

Earth tones and pairs of items enhance life for Kua 2 people.

Auspicious factors for Kua 2

Element	Earth
Color	Red/yellow
Direction	Southwest

130 Unlucky things for Kua 2 people

A diamond brings good luck to Kua 2, but gold on its own may be unlucky.

Everything that is made of metal brings exhausting energy to those with Kua Number 2, and if you wear jewelry it is important to have at least one diamond to bring in the crystal energy. Gold alone might not be so good for you, but when diamonds are added then the jewelry can bring good fortune.

Metallic colors such as gold and silver are bad for your southwest corner, as are dark green and

brown, which are the colors of the Wood element. In fact it is important not to place too many green plants in the southwest direction of your home as this will definitely cause problems for you, bringing obstacles that can even block your success. And if you surround yourself with things made of metal, such as windchimes and bells made of brass, and you place these in the southwest corners of your living or work space, these are sure to weaken you. People who belong to Kua Number 2 always run the risk of being weakened by metallic energies when these are placed in the southwest sector of the house; anywhere else is fine.

Lucky things for Kua 3 people   131

The personalized element energy of those with Kua Number 3 is Big Wood, so having a really beautiful tree in the east sector of your garden will create superb feng shui for you. In the past it was known that trees could bring amazingly auspicious feng shui but the tree in question always had to sync perfectly with the energy of the resident. One method, according to old feng shui lore, was for anyone with Kua Number 3 to have a beautiful tree in the east. So if you are Kua 3 then plant a majestic tree there; the grander and more healthy this tree grows the better will be your feng shui. It is important that the tree grows strong—ensure that it does not wither and die!

Those with Kua 3 also benefit from having a room in the east sector of the house or the east corner of any building as an office. The east brings you benefits because it has a natural affinity with you and if you sit facing east it is likewise beneficial. This is the direction that brings personal growth, making you effective and productive.

The best colors for you are those associated with wood—greens and browns. Thus green emeralds, jade, and tourmalines are excellent. Blue stones such as blue topaz, amethysts, aquamarines, and sapphires are also beneficial.

Auspicious factors for Kua 3 people

Element	Wood
Color	Blue/green
Direction	East

Trees planted in the east are brilliant energizers for Kua 3 people.

Unlucky things for Kua 3 people   132

Things made of metal are dangerous for those with Kua Number 3. Metal and Fire together spell extreme danger so it is a good idea to avoid having these two elements in the east sector of the house. Bright lights bring very exhausting energy to Kua 3, and if you wear red add black to balance it out. You must never wear white with red or gold, as these combinations are sure to hurt your luck.

As for wearing jewelry it is better to wear black silk cords than gold chains. When you wear gold on its own, the energy created in your personal auric space tends to be killing and very exhausting, so refrain from wearing decorative gold chains.

Metallic colors such as gold and silver are bad for your east corner, as are the dark red colors associated with the Fire element. In fact it is important not to make the lights in the east too bright as this is sure to cause problems for you, bringing obstacles that may block your success. So go easy on the bright lights in the east sector. And if you surround yourself in the east corners of your living or work space with things made of metal, such as windchimes and bells made of brass, these are sure to weaken you. People who belong to Kua Number 3 always run the risk of being weakened by metallic energies especially when these are accompanied with red colors.

133 Lucky things for Kua 4 people

Those whose Kua Number is 4 should note that their personalized element energy is Small Wood and that their cosmic force is the wind. Kua 4 people benefit from living in the sectors of their home that are breezy and airy. Their directional location is the southeast, where the element is Wood, symbolized by small plants, flowering shrubs, and fresh flowers rather than by tall, towering trees—so having the kind of plants that can bend with the winds such as bamboo and pines in the southeast is extremely beneficial for Kua 4 people.

Those with Kua 4 also benefit from having their bedroom or office in the southeast corner of any building. The southeast brings benefits because of the natural affinity that Kua 4 people have with this part of the home—and if you sit facing southeast it brings you the luck of wealth and a good name. The wind of the southeast blows

Auspicious factors for Kua 4 people	
Element	Wood
Color	Blue/green
Direction	Southeast

Green gemstones, such as emerald and jade, are lucky for Kua 4 people.

auspiciously for you and this is the direction that brings personal growth, attracting success and recognition for you.

Focus on green
The best colors for you as a Kua 4 person are the lighter greens and the deeper blues. Green gemstones are excellent, such as emeralds and jade, though green tourmalines are less suitable for Kua 4 people. Blue stones are also beneficial and these include blue topaz, aquamarines, and sapphires; amethysts are also excellent. Remember that for you the best things have a blue-green overtone, so blue or green amber is amazingly lucky for you—if you can find this rare stone.

You will also benefit from having some kind of water feature in the southeast, as Water here helps Wood to flourish and grow.

134 Unlucky things for Kua 4 people

Gems for Kua 4 people

As with Kua 3 people, Kua 4 people are also averse to all things made of metal. Metal and Fire together signify danger, so it is an excellent idea to ensure that the southeast sector of your house is not overly lit. Bright lights situated in the southeast corner are sure to bring obstacles that block your success.

Bright lights exhaust the energy of those with Kua Number 4, so it is not a good idea to wear too much red, or have excessive amount of red clothes inside your wardrobe. Red is a color that is both unfriendly and dangerous for you, and definitely will not bring you much luck at all.

With jewelry it is better to wear black silk cords and to avoid wearing gold chains. Gold on its own does all things negative to you as the energy created is too strong, but add diamonds and colored stones and the energy transforms into something auspicious for you Kua 4 people! Metallic colors such as gold and silver are also bad for your southeast corner, as are the dark red colors of the Fire element. Nor should there be metallic furniture here—its presence would be sure to cause problems for you.

Lucky and unlucky things for Kua 5 people

Everything that is made of metal brings exhausting energy to those with Kua Number 5, and this is because the Metal element brings depleting vibes to the Earth chi of number 5 people. This is a powerful Earth element number that has special strength during the current Period of 8 and it is also a number that brings misfortunes to everyone. However, if you are Kua 5, the number 5 in the charts has the potential to bring you transformational luck, the kind that can turn negative energies into positive.

Women with Kua 5 have the same attributes as those with Kua 8, while men with Kua 5 follow those with Kua 2 so you can read the sections on these two Kua Numbers to gain greater insights into your Kua Number depending on your gender.

The strength of Earth

Those with Kua 5 are naturally strong Earth people who benefit hugely from the presence of crystals around them, and the older these crystals are the better; they also benefit from wearing lots of colored gemstones and these must be natural and mined from the ground—citrines and amethysts being especially nourishing for Kua 5 people.

What is also good for Kua 5 people is bright fiery red energy—the power of the Fire element strengthens and empowers the chi strength of 5: if you wear red you will attract success easily and effortlessly. A good idea is to place a bright chandelier in the middle of the home to activate the power of the original 5 of the Lo Shu square.

Auspicious factors for Kua 5 people	
Element	Earth
Color	Red/yellow
Direction	Men: Southwest
	Women: Northeast

Wearing red and having bright lights and candle flames attracts the energy of Fire, which brings success to Kua 5 people. As Kua 5s are linked also with the Earth element, they benefit greatly from the presence of crystals, such as citrine (left) and amethyst (right).

136 Lucky things for Kua 6 people

Everything that is made of metal—gold and silver—brings excellent energy to those with Kua Number 6, and if you wear jewelry, the thicker the gold the better. Kua 6 people are energized by the Metal element so for them gold and fine jewelry does a great deal indeed. Wearing jewelry is definitely very lucky for you.

Auspicious factors for Kua 6 people

Element	Metal
Color	Yellow/white
Direction	Northwest

You also benefit from wearing white and metallic colors such as gold and silver and your northwest corner should be painted white to maintain the strength of the pure white energy here. Kua 6 people are best located in the northwest corner and this is the sector that also stands for the patriarch and for heavenly energy. Locating your bedroom here is excellent feng shui for you... It is also good to activate the northwest with auspicious symbols of good fortune, all done in brass or metal.

Another good element for the northwest will be the Earth element since this produces the element of the sector. So earthy colors are extremely suitable for the northwest corner.

Surrounding yourself with things made of metal such as windchimes and bells made of brass and placing them in the northwest corners of your living or workspace is sure to strengthen you.

A bedroom in the northwest of your home decorated in earth colors brings excellent luck for Kua 6 people.

137 Unlucky things for Kua 6 people

Things that suggest Fire element energy are dangerous for those with Kua Number 6 because Fire consumes Metal energy, spelling extreme danger. It is a good idea to avoid having excessively bright lighting, a fireplace, or the kitchen in the northwest part of the house. These are harmful from a feng shui perspective and are more so for those whose Kua Number is 6. The northwest is associated with heaven, so having Fire here is like having fire at heaven's gate.

Bright lights bring destructive energy to those with Kua Number 6, and if you wear red it is important

to add black to balance out the red. You must never wear red on its own as this simply brings killing energy towards your persona. Red as a color choice is sure to hurt your luck.

It is better to wear gold chains than silk cords. Wearing gold on its own empowers the energy in your personal auric space and when you add diamonds your luck will increase even more.

Gold enhanced with diamonds boosts luck; silk cords deplete it.

Lucky things for Kua 7 people

138

Kua 7 people are also energized by the Metal element so that everything that is made of metal will enhance your energy, attracting strength, success, and prosperity. The number 7 was very strong during the Period of 7 but now that it has been replaced by the Period of 8 it has lost much of its luster and its strength.

As such, what is needed for Kua 7 people is to activate the power of 7. You can do this by hanging a large metallic bell in the west and hitting the bell on a daily basis. This introduces much needed yang chi for the west. If you can, try

Auspicious factors for Kua 7 people

Element	Metal
Color	Yellow/white
Direction	West

Placing a metallic bell in the west helps Kua 7s.

to make these bells give off a lingering sound— the kind that monks in Tibet and Nepal use to strengthen their meditations. Even if your bell cannot give off a tuneful sound placing it in the west is still extremely beneficial.

Use gold to boost success
Those of you who like wearing jewelry to enhance your personal feng shui are sure to be pleased to hear that this is indeed the best recommendation for Kua 7 people. The more gold you wear the better will be your success luck. Kua 7 people are energized by the Metal element so for them gold and fine jewelry does a great deal indeed.

You also benefit from wearing white and metallic colors such as gold and silver and your west corner should be painted white to activate its own Metal element. In the west, crystals are also excellent because Earth is the sector's element, making earthy colors suitable for you and the sector.

Unlucky things for Kua 7 people

139

Kua 7 people must avoid being too closely allied to the Fire and Water elements which can sap you of your strength and energy, and cause your good fortune luck to leak out, so do be careful with the lighting of your home. You must also not place water in the west as this is sure to hurt you.

Things that suggest Fire element energy are dangerous for those with Kua Number 7 and this is because Fire consumes Metal energy, causing it to dissolve and melt. Avoid having bright lights or a fireplace in the west. Another thing to avoid here is water as it depletes the energy of Metal. Avoid the colors blue and black here as carefully as you avoid red.

It is vital that you never wear dark blue gemstones such as sapphires or lapis—these will cause you to

lose your luck. In fact, avoid all kinds of blue stone. As for clothes, Kua 7 people should avoid wearing too much black which is one of the most harmful colors for those who belong to Kua 7.

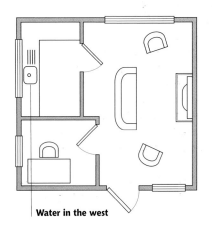

Check out the placement of Fire, such as a fireplace, and Water in your home, in terms of water features, sinks, and bathrooms.

Water in the west

140 Lucky things for Kua 8 people

As we are currently in the Period of 8 those whose Kua Number is 8 are sure to enjoy some exceptional luck all the way through to 2024. As we move deeper into the period, those with this Kua Number will feel its benevolent energy even more.

Knowing all the things that bring you luck can help you double your luck and, in fact, it is worthwhile to go to a great deal of trouble to activate and energize your northeast location with Earth element energy—the kind that is sure to attract good fortune vibes for you. It would benefit you to make the northeast your personal space, so activate it by making certain it is well-lit as Fire energy will strengthen your Earth chi.

Auspicious factors for Kua 8 people	
Element	Earth
Color	Red/yellow
Direction	Northeast

Another must-have for the northeast is a picture or painting of a big mountain range. Supplement this with a large crystal geode—this will bring in the power of the great

Meanwhile the best color for Kua 8 people are the earth tones—from yellow to golden although red is also very suitable. Earth tones have the best natural affinity for you.

Earth energy—or place a globe image or solid crystal or glass balls here.

Utilize the Period of 8

Remember that the northeast is the sector of the current Period of 8. It is a west-group direction and location and it is also an axis direction so is extremely powerful. The best thing you can do if your Kua Number is 8 is to stay here and then energize the power of 8 with a crystal 8 containing specks of gold.

141 Unlucky things for Kua 8 people

Everything that is made of metal brings exhausting energy to those with Kua Number 8, and if you wear jewelry it is important to have at least one diamond so that its powerful energy will let the Earth chi stay in control.

The color white, as well as all kinds of metallic colors, are bad for your northeast corner, as are dark green and brown, which are the colors of the Wood element. In fact, it is important not to place too many green plants in the northeast location of your home as this will cause problems for you, bringing obstacles that block your success. So go

easy on the plants in the northeast sector and if you would naturally like to surround yourself in your living or work space with things made of metal such as windchimes and bells, resist the urge as these will sap you of your strength. People who belong to Kua Number 8 always run the risk of being weakened by metallic energies when these are placed in the northeast sector of the house. Anywhere else is fine.

Diamonds protect Kua 8 people against the exhausting influence of metal.

Lucky things for Kua 9 people

142

Kua Number 9 can bring you the power of the element of Fire. The number 9 also signifies future prosperity, so those of you who belong to Kua 9 should immediately note your auspicious east-group directions and simultaneously create an oasis of red, fiery energy located in the south sector of your home. In this way, you will be activating the number 9 and tapping into its

Red brings success for Kua 9 people, so have lots of it in the south of your home to energize your luck.

current strong energy at the same time.

So, what is good for Kua 9 people? Basically, anything that suggests the Fire element, so things that are bright, to do with sunshine, and the color red. The element of Wood is also excellent so everything that grows—which means healthy, growing plants—can symbolically and cosmically feed and strengthen Fire element energy.

Auspicious factors for Kua 9 people	
Element	Fire
Color	Green/red
Direction	South

Emphasize red

In the south, which is the direction of the number, have red curtains or carpets, or paint the walls here bright red! Also display lots of healthy plants and blooming flowers.

The south is the place of the horse and the phoenix—both bring excellent recognition luck. For speedy success, place a symbolic nine-horses ornament here, and for opportunities that increase your net worth, place nine phoenixes in the south.

Unlucky things for Kua 9 people

143

Water may not be so helpful in the south. Fire and Water elements clash directly, so it is best not to have excessive amounts of water here. A water feature such as a pond, a pool, or an aquarium can have the effect of putting Fire out, so it is usually best to keep water well away from the south of a property.

Another element that could hurt and exhaust Fire energy is the element of Earth, so crystals and other Earth element objects should not be placed in the south. Earth exhausts Fire and this presence in excess in the south will create blockages to your energy here.

Wood energy is fine in the south, as it supports Fire in the five-element cycle.

144 Feng shui astrology—directions and animal signs

A very easy method of practicing instant feng shui astrology is to study the astrology wheel, which shows where each of the 12 Chinese animal signs has its direction. In the Chinese calendar, the animal signs are known as the earthly branches of the year, and they each have a matching compass direction. Thus, depending on your animal sign, you will have a direction location in the house that corresponds to you and your luck.

Finding your direction

Once you find your direction, you must ensure that neither a toilet nor a storeroom is located there, otherwise your personal luck will be afflicted. The easiest way to find your direction is to determine your animal sign based on your year of birth (see opposite), then check the astrology wheel shown here. Note that each animal sign is allotted a 15° segment of the compass direction The four cardinal

directions, South, North, East, and West, are represented by one animal sign each—the horse, rat, rabbit, and rooster, respectively. The secondary directions, Southwest, Northwest, Southeast, and Northeast, have two animal signs each.

To make the most of this method of optimizing the feng shui of everybody in your home, you should go on to identify the personalized astrological direction of all residents and then neutralize all negative afflictions in those directions while enhancing the relevant corners with the correct energizing symbols.

There are twelve animal signs in the Chinese zodiac: the Rat, Ox, Tiger, Rabbit, Dragon, Snake, Horse, Sheep, Monkey, Rooster, Dog, and Boar. Each occupies 15° of the compass. It is good feng shui to ensure that the direction that corresponds to your sign is neither missing nor afflicted, and instead has many auspicious objects to energize the sector for you.

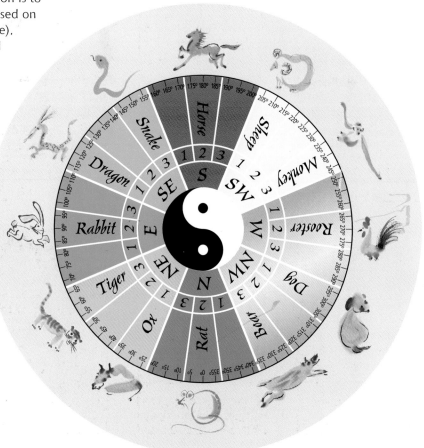

FENG SHUI FORMULAS FOR A HAPPY HOME

FIND YOUR CHINESE ASTROLOGY ANIMAL SIGN

RAT	OX	TIGER	RABBIT
18 Feb 1912 – 5 Feb 1913	6 Feb 1913 – 25 Jan 1914	26 Jan 1914 – 13 Feb 1915	14 Feb 1915 – 2 Feb 1916
5 Feb 1924 – 23 Jan 1925	24 Jan 1925 – 12 Feb 1926	13 Feb 1926 – 1 Feb 1927	2 Feb 1927 – 22 Jan 1928
24 Jan 1936 – 10 Feb 1937	11 Feb 1937 – 30 Jan 1938	31 Jan 1938 – 18 Feb 1939	19 Feb 1939 – 7 Feb 1940
10 Feb 1948 – 28 Jan 1949	29 Jan 1949 – 16 Feb 1950	17 Feb 1950 – 5 Feb 1951	6 Feb 1951– 26 Jan 1952
28 Jan 1960 – 14 Feb 1961	15 Feb 1961 – 4 feb 1962	5 Feb 1962 – 24 Jan 1963	25 Jan 1963 – 12 Feb 1964
15 Feb 1972 – 2 Feb 1973	3 Feb 1973 – 22 Jan 1974	23 Jan 1974 – 10 Feb 1975	11 Feb 1975 – 30 Jan 1976
2 Feb 1984 – 19 Feb 1985	20 Feb 1985 – 8 Feb 1986	9 Feb 1986 – 28 Jan 1987	29 Jan 1987 – 16 Feb 1998
19 Feb 1996 – 6 Feb 1997	7 Feb 1997 – 27 Jan 1998	28 Jan 1998 – 15 Feb 1999	16 Feb 1999 – 4 Feb 2000
7 Feb 2008 – 25 Jan 2009	26 Jan 2009 –13 Feb 2010	14 Feb 2010 – 2 Feb 2011	3 Feb 2011 – 22 Jan 2012

DRAGON	SNAKE	HORSE	SHEEP
3 Feb 1916 – 22 Jan 1917	23 Jan 1917 –10 Feb 1918	11 Feb 1918 – 31 Jan 1919	1 Feb 1919 – 19 Feb 1920
23 Jan 1928 – 9 Feb 1929	10 Feb 1929 – 29 Jan 1930	30 Jan 1930 – 16 Feb 1931	17 Feb 1931 – 5 Feb 1932
8 Feb 1940 – 26 Jan 1941	27 Jan 1941 – 14 Feb 1942	15 Feb 1942 – 4 Feb 1943	5 Feb 1943 – 24 Jan 1944
27 Jan 1952 – 13 Feb 1953	14 Feb 1953 – 2 Feb 1954	3 Feb 1954 – 23 Jan 1955	24 Jan 1955 – 11 Fen 1956
13 Feb 1964 – 1 Feb 1965	2 Feb 1965 – 20 Jan 1966	21 Jan 1966 – 8 Feb 1967	9 Feb 1967 – 29 Jan 1968
31 Jan 1976 – 17 Feb 1977	18 Feb 1977 – 6 Feb 1978	7 Feb 1978 – 27 Jan 1979	28 Jan 1979 – 15 Feb 1980
17 Feb 1988 – 5 Feb 1989	6 Feb 1989 – 26 Jan 1990	27 Jan 1990 – 14 Feb 1991	15 Feb 1991 – 3 Feb 1992
5 Feb 2000 – 23 Jan 2001	24 Jan 2001 – 11 Feb 2002	12 Feb 2002 – 31 Jan 2003	1 Feb 2003 – 21 Jan 2004
23 Jan 2012 – 9 Feb 2013	10 Feb 2013 – 30 Jan 2014	31 Jan 2014 – 18 Feb 2015	19 Feb 2015 – 7 Feb 2016

MONKEY	ROOSTER	DOG	BOAR
20 Feb 1920 – 7 Feb 1921	8 Feb 1921 – 27 Jan 1922	28 Jan 1922 – 15 Feb 1923	16 Feb 1923 – 4 Feb 1924
6 Feb 1932 – 25 Jan 1933	26 Jan 1933 – 13 Feb 1934	14 Feb 1934 – 3 Feb 1935	4 Feb 1935 – 23 Jan 1936
25 Jan 1944 – 12 Feb 1945	13 Feb 1945 – 1 Feb 1946	2 Jan 1946 – 21 Jan 1947	22 Jan 1947 – 9 Feb 1948
12 Feb 1956 – 30 Jan 1957	31 Jan 1957 – 17 Feb 1958	18 Feb 1958 – 7 Feb 1959	8 Feb 1959 – 27 Jan 1960
30 Jan 1968 – 16 Feb 1969	17 Feb 1969 – 5 Feb 1970	6 Feb 1970 – 26 Jan 1971	27 Jan 1971 – 14 Feb 1972
16 Feb 1980 – 4 Feb 1981	5 Feb 1981 – 24 Jan 1982	25 Jan 1982 – 12 Feb 1983	13 Feb 1983 – 1 Feb 1984
4 Feb 1992 – 22 Jan 1993	23 Jan 1993 – 9 Feb 1994	10 Feb 1994 – 30 Jan 1995	31 Jan 1995 – 18 Feb 1996
22 Jan 2004 – 8 Feb 2005	9 Feb 2005 – 28 Jan 2006	29 Jan 2006 – 17 Feb 2007	18 Fen 2007 – 6 Feb 2008
8 Feb 2016 – 27 Jan 2017	28 Jan 2017 – 15 Feb 2018	16 Feb 2018 – 4 Feb 2019	5 Feb 2019 – 24 Jan 2020

145 Activate your animal-sign direction to improve personal luck

Once you find the location that corresponds to your animal sign, maximize your luck by strengthening the chi of that area. If there is a toilet or a storeroom occupying this direction, however, do not activate it—the chi is afflicted or locked up and is doing you no good at all.

Activating your luck

The best way to activate for good things to come into your life is to use energizing images of your own astrological animal sign surrounded by wish-fulfilling jewels, which are cut crystals. It is best to use animal images made from natural crystal, such as quartz, agates, tourmaline, jade, and so forth. These natural treasures from deep within the earth contain very concentrated chi. When surrounded by wish-fulfilling jewels and positioned in your office or on your desk in the

direction of your astrology sign, the chi becomes very engaged with your personal energy. Choose crystal colors as follows:

- Yellow cut crystals, cush as citrine, for wealth wishes

- Pink cut crystals, such as ruby or rose quartz, for love-related wishes

- Blue cut crystals, such as blue chalcedony, for healing wishes

- Green cut crystals, such as peridot or emerald for expansion and growth

- Lavender cut crystals, such as amethyst, for personal growth and development.

Finding your astro-compass sector

ANIMAL SIGN	COMPASS BEARING	COMPASS SECTOR
Rat	352.5°–7.5°	North 2
Ox	22.5°–37.5°	Northeast 1
Tiger	52.5°–67.5°	Northeast 3
Rabbit	82.5°–97.5°	East 2
Dragon	112.5°–127.5°	Southeast 1
Snake	142.5°–157.5°	Southeast 3
Horse	172.5°–187.5°	South 2
Sheep	202.5°–217.5°	Southwest 1
Monkey	232.5°–247.5°	Southwest 3
Rooster	262.5°–277.5°	West 2
Dog	292.5°–307.5°	Northwest 1
Boar	322.5°–337.5°	Northwest 3

Note the compass direction associated with your animal sign, then place an image of your animal in the corresponding sector of your home. Displaying your animal with gemstones adds to its power to bring you auspicious luck.

Four friends of the astrology zodiac

146

More than the trinity is the foursome in Taoist good-fortune reckonings. Thus Chinese astrological systems always stress the groups of four that make up the special foursome in the astrological good-fortune stakes. This refers to animal signs that are particularly good for one another, so that knowing which of the three sets of four animal groupings you belong to enables you not only to differentiate between those who are your friends and those who may not be, but also enables you to activate your space with auspicious images from the animal zodiac that are beneficial for you. Check the chart opposite to discover your special astrological allies, and your "secret friend"—the one whose help and assistance may not be so obvious to you.

Your allies and secret friend

To become knowledgeable about your friends and allies just see the groupings here and commit them to memory.

Animal sign	Three zodiac allies	One secret friend
Rat	rat plus dragon & monkey	ox
Ox	ox plus snake & rooster	rat
Tiger	tiger plus horse & dog	boar
Rabbit	rabbit plus sheep & boar	dog
Dragon	dragon plus rat & monkey	rooster
Snake	snake plus rooster & ox	monkey
Horse	horse plus tiger & dog	sheep
Sheep	sheep plus rabbit & boar	horse
Monkey	monkey plus dragon & rat	snake
Rooster	rooster plus snake & ox	dragon
Dog	dog plus horse & tiger	rabbit
Boar	boar plus sheep & rabbit	tiger

Helpful and unhelpful people

The Chinese are always so sensitive about whether people are "helpful" or "unhelpful" in an astrological context, even having special names to describe them. So, for instance, those unhelpful or harmful are often described as the "devil people in your life." Good luck always refers to mentors coming into your life to help you, while one of the worst kinds of misfortune luck is often described as meeting up with "devil people," or those who would cause you harm and therefore should always be avoided.

Each animal has two allies in Chinese astrology. The dog's allies are the horse and the tiger. His secret friend is the rabbit. Looking up your allies helps identify your true friends in life.

Secret friend

147 Avoid your natural zodiac enemies

You must be very mindful that the astrological wheel also alerts you to your natural astrological foes, and it is imperative you do not display their image in your direction. Thus, for example, the dog and dragon are natural enemies, so it is important not to display the dragon image in the direction that corresponds to that of the dog—in other words, do not place the dragon in the Northwest 1 direction.

To draw the energy of the dragon, which is one of the most auspicious of symbols, into your house place the dragon in his own Southeast direction or in the East or North. In any case, the dragon is a special circumstance as he is so powerful.

Those born in the dog year should also be aware that it is perfectly acceptable to wear a dragon image and that, in fact, it is advisable to do so. By doing this, the dragon image takes on the energy of a talisman, bringing protection and luck.

148 Three seasonal animals of astrology

In addition to the zodiac alliances shown in Tip 146, there is another trinity of astrological signs that also point to auspicious energy being created through the chi changes that transform luck from season to season. It is thus useful to note that there are four groupings to signify the four seasons, with each group comprising three animal signs, as shown on the chart below. When they are present within the same family they generate a great deal of special luck energy during the season they represent. The best combination consists of the mother, the father, and one child.

Wintertime is auspicious for the rat, boar, and ox.

The seasonality grouping of animal signs are as follows:

Spring	dragon, rabbit, and tiger
Summer	horse, snake, and sheep
Fall	rooster, dog, and monkey
Winter	rat, boar, and ox

Watching out for astrological afflictions in the home

149

It is beneficial to use the astrological wheel (see Tip 144) to clear your home systematically of astrological afflictions. This means investigating the spaces that represent the personal astrology spaces of every single member of the family living there. Look out for physical afflictions, such as beams and sharp edges pointing to identified corners, and make a special effort to neutralize them. For example, if the patriarch of the family is a horse person then you must make sure that the South (which is the horse direction) is not hurt by anything sharp or pointed. The South should also not be locked up, nor should there be a toilet or a kitchen in the South as these press down on the horse person's good fortune.

Avoiding your enemies

In the same way, also ensure that the directions of all family members are not inadvertently made dangerous by having images of their astrological enemies placed in them. The remedy here is simply to place these symbols elsewhere. Understand that astrological enemies are dangerous only when they are placed in the home direction of a resident. Placed anywhere else, and they are perfectly safe. As an example

of this, although the rat and horse are enemies, as long as the horse image is not placed in the North (the Rat's direction), and it is placed in its own direction of the South, the horse can bring enormous good fortune to the rat-born resident.

The Southwest 3 direction is the animal-sign direction of the Monkey. Don't place a Tiger in this location, as the Monkey and Tiger are astrological enemies. Place the Tiger in his own natural sector, which is Northeast 3.

150 Carry images of your secret friend to invoke sincere friendship

One of the easiest and most effective way of ensuring good personalized feng shui based on your astrology chart is simply to carry images of your allies and secret friends (see Tip 146). This is something known to the Chinese since forever, and it is the reason why there are always so many images of the 12 astrological animal signs.

The best way to wear them is on a charm bracelet. Each person should wear a minimum of three—although four are best—animal signs, made up of the three animals that represent your affinity animals as well as your secret friend.

An Ox person will benefit from wearing images of the rooster, snake, ox, and rat.

Know your affinity animals and friends

1 **A dragon person** will benefit from wearing a charm bracelet with the monkey, rat, dragon, and rooster.
2 **A monkey person** will benefit from wearing a charm bracelet with the monkey, rat, dragon, and snake.
3 **A rat person** will benefit from wearing a charm bracelet with the monkey, rat, dragon, and ox.
4 **A snake person** will benefit from wearing a charm bracelet with the rooster, snake, ox, and monkey.
5 **A rooster person** will benefit from wearing a charm bracelet with the rooster, snake, ox, and dragon.
6 **An ox person** will benefit from wearing a charm bracelet with the rooster, snake, ox, and rat.
7 **A boar person** will benefit from wearing a charm bracelet with the boar, sheep, rabbit, and tiger.
8 **A sheep person** will benefit from wearing a charm bracelet with the boar, sheep, rabbit, and horse.
9 **A rabbit person** will benefit from wearing a charm bracelet with the boar, sheep, rabbit, and dog.
10 **A dog person** will benefit from wearing a charm bracelet with the dog, horse, tiger, and rabbit.
11 **A horse person** will benefit from wearing a charm bracelet with the dog, horse, tiger, and sheep.
12 **A tiger person** will benefit from wearing a charm bracelet with the dog, horse, tiger, and boar.

Charm bracelets displaying Chinese animals activate the protection of your astrological allies.

Strengthen the element of your animal sign 151

The final activity related to astrological feng shui is to take note of the element of your animal sign and to strengthen its home location by placing something of the producing element there. For example, the dragon, sheep, ox, and dog are described as having the earth element.

Animal elements
• The sheep and the ox are already residing in earth locations; the dragon, however, resides in a wood location, which makes it weak. It is a good idea to strengthen the dragon location of Southeast 1 with fire energy. This will enhance the chi essence of the dragon. The dog is located in the Northwest 1 location, which is metal. This exhausts the dog so the Northwest 1 dog direction should also be enhanced with fire energy.

• The rooster and monkey are both intrinsically metal. The rooster is in the West so it is strong enough and the monkey is in the Southwest, which makes it even stronger. For these two animal signs, there is no need to do anything more.

• The snake and the horse are both fire element. The horse is located in the South, whose element is also fire, so the horse is fine. But the snake is even better, because it is located in the Southeast, which is wood. So for these two animal signs, there is no need to do anything more.

You can bring the fire element into a room by introducing reds and oranges into the decor.

• The tiger and the rabbit are both wood element. Note that the tiger is located in the Northeast, which is earth. Wood overcomes earth, but it is distracted. It is necessary to strengthen the tiger with water energy. So placing water here would benefit anyone who is born in the year of the tiger. The rabbit meanwhile is in the East, which is also wood, so the rabbit is fine. There is no need to do anything more.

• The rat and the pig—or boar—are both water element. The rat is in the North, which is also water, so there is no need to do anything more. The pig is in the Northwest 3 direction, which is metal, where it is being enhanced, so again there is no need to do anything.

In Chinese astrology, the boar, or pig's, associated element is water, and his compass direction is Northwest 3.

152 The four cardinal directions

The four cardinal directions—north, south, east, and west—are represented by the rat, the rabbit, the horse, and the rooster. In Chinese feng shui, however, these four directions are so powerful that houses are deliberately oriented just a little bit off the four cardinal directions—throughout history only temples and palaces have been felt to be suitable to face exactly north, south, east, or west.

However, the four cardinal directions are vital sectors of any home and they should be carefully energized by placing either the astrological animal signs or, better yet, the relevant one of the four celestial guardians.

In addition to the four celestial creatures there are also the all-powerful Four Heavenly Kings—these are Buddhist deities that over the centuries have found their way into feng shui legend mainly because they are such fearsome and effective protectors. The Four Heavenly Kings protect households against falling victim to physical disaster—floods, fires, hurricanes, earthquakes, viruses, epidemics, and all other calamities, both natural and manmade. These attributes make them extremely relevant these days when the world seems to be rocked with so many natural disasters brought by wind, rain, and fire... As such there has been a big revival in their popularity as the four most powerful of home guardians.

Find the right guardian for each sector

Placing a set of celestials activates the guardianship of these exceptional feng shui creatures—their chi energy is what brings good fortune to the home. Use the following celestial creature in each sector:

East	dragon
South	phoenix
North	tortoise
West	tiger

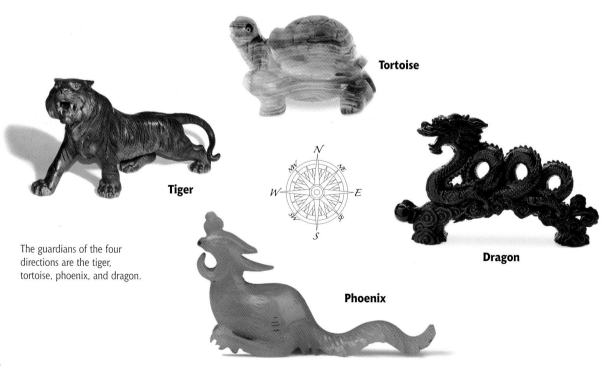

Tortoise

Tiger

Dragon

Phoenix

The guardians of the four directions are the tiger, tortoise, phoenix, and dragon.

Chapter Three

Transforming Your Thought Energy

The power of your personal feng shui can have as important an impact on your life as the physical feng shui of your home. Work at creating channels for the inner spirituality within you to flow outwards, adding to your charisma, making you more attractive and giving your words greater power. Moreover, the special energy unleashed will dispel negatives such as depression, selfishness and anger.

You can also use feng shui secrets to enhance your physical and spiritual health, giving you good looks and a strong body. The same secrets can also increase the strength of your aura and personal magnetism, attracting happiness and easy success.

By activating the power that lies within all of us you can liberate and empower your mind, maximizing your potential for success a thousandfold.

153 Engage your inner spiritual power and tune in mentally

As all knowledge, all experiences, and all our life's outcomes emanate from the mind, the most effective practitioners of feng shui are not necessarily the most learned or the oldest, they are the most experienced and the humblest and they recognize and use the power of their own minds.

I have discovered over many years of observation that the most effective feng shui masters are no different from successful professionals in other fields of endeavor—they are always the ones who are the most relaxed and the most humble—but they also possess a quiet and reassuring steely confidence that comes from deep within them.

These were the Taoist masters I was most fortunate to meet and closely observe doing their work. They were not necessarily particularly famous but amongst a private circle of feng shui masters they were highly respected.

Spiritual clarity

The Taoist feng shui masters of Hong Kong were deeply spiritual, although when you first met them you might not have thought so. They were master meditators whose minds were powerful and clear. They were always relaxed and always good-humoured, and when they made recommendations to clients, it would be obvious that they could accurately see the end result of their recommendation in their mind. They described what had to be done as though it were a picture that they could see with absolute clarity.

In the process they seemed to be imbuing their advice with an inner spiritual power, which later I was to discover we can all harness in the same way.

Delve into your mind

The secret lies in going deep into your mind and engaging your spiritual potential to add a kind of divine strength to your actions. The magic "open sesame" lies in the purity of your motivation: when feng shui is practised with genuine good intentions to benefit the people living within a home, it takes on great power. This chapter is devoted to introducing the ideas of delving far into your subconscious.

Start by learning how to delve into the depths of your own consciousness with simple meditation exercises that let the chi flow into your body.

ENERGY TIP

Meditate daily to gain inner awareness

Close your eyes to shut out distractions, breathe normally, stay relaxed, and then direct your mind to go deep inside yourself. Do this for a few moments each day until you become familiar with the exercise. It will soon help you rest your mind and make it clearer, opening the inner depths of your mind, your own thought processes to you.

Spiritual means the mind—try to understand its potential   154

The word "spiritual" refers to the mind, and spiritual people are those who seek to maximize the mind's potential. When you understand that it is your own mind that has complete and ultimate control over everything that happens to you, your chi, and your space, you will come to understand the far-reaching consequences of your belief systems, your attitudes, behavior, actions, speech, and responses. Both singly and collectively these have an effect on the outcome of all your actions. But the space you live in and the chi that surrounds you also influence your life, so your mind must be harnessed to enhance the arrangement and design of your surroundings.

The power of yin

This practice of inner feng shui is also referred to as "the power of yin—the silent inner reaches of the mind." Yin—as in yin and yang—always features strongly when one taps into the potential of the inner divine self, which is, of course, simply another way of describing the mind.

When your mind is positive everything you do to improve the feng shui of your space will be strengthened and made a thousand times more effective. When you add on the empowering strength of your mind, the effects get magnified even more.

Thus, something as simple as placing a symbolic object in a certain corner of your home is sure to take on greater power to bring you new success when accompanied with a powerful inner intention, helping empower something that is already cosmically correct. Imagine how powerful that can be!

Rise above your own negativities

When you begin to really believe in the power of your mind to enhance your practice of feng shui, any lingering depression is spontaneously

Calm your mind by inviting a holy object such as this Buddha figure into your home. The best place for such a statue is in the northwest of any room.

dispelled. Failure instantly becomes a thing of the past and all afflictions caused by outer cosmic forces can be overcome by the power of your own positive thinking.

When you know you can rise above the negativities of the environment around you, and that there are simply no limits to your power over intangible afflictions, you have started practising inner feng shui. This added dimension of your use of feng shui is certain to magnify the potency of the ancient practice of space enhancement a thousandfold.

TRANSFORMING YOUR THOUGHT ENERGY

155 Dejunking the mind of clutter

Alas, we have huge amounts of clutter inside our heads, collected through the years, consciously and unconsciously, along the journey of life. We store junk-thoughts in the mind's various compartments from the moment we are born and, because the mind has an all-powerful supercharged storehouse capability, we are not aware of all the surplus information stored within. Over time, we accumulate sad experiences that reinforce negative attitudes. These do little good to our sense of well-being and state of mind. Depressing memories that are reinforced over time lead to frustration, anger, jealousy, harmful attachments, stress, and possibly fears and phobias. We will be happier as individuals if we reduce the intensity and quantity of our mental garbage and, even better, eliminate it altogether. This will result in a lightening of the load that confuses the brain, and negates our ability to remain rational, composed, and happy.

What leads to mental decluttering?

Mental junk needs clearing even more than physical junk. But clearing physical junk is what starts the overall dejunking process that affects the mind. It acts as a catalyst.

Thousands of volumes have been written about the memory storehouse of the human mind, including research into our retentive capability, the conscious and subconscious, the way we recall and use information, and, most importantly, how our behavior and attitudes are directly and indirectly influenced by everything we have ever experienced, seen, heard,

Every day we absorb a barrage of useful and useless information that accumulates as negative mental clutter.

learned, and digested. It is believed that the mind is so powerful that it forgets nothing. And if we believe all that is currently emerging about past lives and people's memories of them, it seems that the mind also does not forget anything it has experienced in other lives. This means that it is not easy to clear negativity from the mind.

Moreover, when we consider the sheer volume of information stored here–experiences, feelings, attitudes—surely what we have in our homes is really nothing when compared to the clutter inside our minds.

Ritual for mental dejunking

Close your eyes (without falling asleep) and tune into your mind. Observe the thoughts that flow through it. Watching the mind will make you aware of the number of random thoughts that weave their way in and out of your consciousness. Do this each time you feel angry, frustrated, or stressed. Do it each time the name of someone important to you crops up, or an issue you are debating is being discussed. Watch your mind and get a feeling for what's inside it. Try this also while trying to study, work, or concentrate. You will be surprised at the amount of junk-thoughts that interrupt your thinking. Dejunking the mind of negative and irrelevant thoughts enhances concentration and reduces your tension and fears. Make a conscious decision to do this, because it will bring emotional liberation that leads to a less stressful and aggravating life.

Cleansing the mind of attitude clutter

The biggest hurdle to clearing the mind of harmful negative phobias is the self-realization that must precede the clearing. Once you think things through in your mind and are able to admit to your fears, there is seldom a need for anyone else to be aware of, or even to participate in, your mental clearing exercises. However, there will be those who will benefit from a guide or therapist who, through directed thought processes, can lead you through the different stages of mind cleansing and help you to admit that you do have fears, which will simply evaporate once you realize you have them.

Clearing attitude clutter

Like spiritually charged negative energy, which takes so much effort to dislodge and cleanse from your mind completely, behavioral phobias are also deeply entrenched in you and therefore, cannot be cleared from your mind overnight. However, once you begin to become self-aware, accepting your vulnerability allows the cleansing of attitude clutter to get underway. Fear of pain, anger, rejection, and frustration become part of life and living.

A yang attitude encourages friendships based on openness and positivity.

Difficult situations and relationships become things not to be feared but ones to be managed and overcome. Looking at relationships and situations this way requires a shift in attitude, and this can happen only when negative self-destructive attitudes are thrown away, eliminated, discarded and washed off.

Getting a yang attitude

Attitude is something that can apply to every single thing that happens to us. The yin and yang of attitude is but the two faces of the same situation, the same person. It is entirely up to us which side we want to see and react to, and which side of our attitude we want to react with. Even

when we see the situation or person we are interacting with as yin, we can still react positively in a yang way. When we make a habit of always reacting in a yang manner, we are setting up a yang bonding pattern for the future and discarding the yin bonding pattern.

Yang bonding patterns are very revitalizing. They open doorways to opportunities and positive relationships. Yin bonding patterns, on the other hand, close the doors to these developments. They create enemies and make situations worse. They cause more clutter to build up within the mind, clutter that reinforces self-destructive responses and bonding patterns.

TRANSFORMING YOUR THOUGHT ENERGY

157 Affirmations to re-energize self-esteem

I have been a firm believer in affirmations for as long as I can remember. Early on, I discovered that if I wanted something to happen badly enough, if I kept saying it, repeating it, and thinking about it in a positive way, it would miraculously manifest. In the same way, if I wanted to develop a certain skill or ability, I would single-mindedly affirm my desire in my mind, and somehow situations would conspire for me to acquire the knowledge or experience I yearned for.

This was how I found myself the owner and chairman of my own department store in Hong Kong during the mid-eighties. I had discovered that I had a weakness for shopping and I realized that shopping was fun only when one has loads of money. But my subconscious mind was smarter. It propelled me into packaging the kind of investment banking deal I had been doing for years as part of my job, to enable me to acquire a department store. For two years, I shopped like an empress for my thirteen stores. It was amazing. When I tired of that life, I cashed in by selling out.

Later, when I discovered mantras and found that yogis and lamas spend their lives chanting holy mantras in their quest for a transformation of the mind, and for enlightenment, my belief in affirmations was strengthened a thousandfold. Since then, I have turned my affirmations towards less material goals and more towards spiritual empowerments. I am also very keen now to transform my mind.

If you want to empower your own aura, it is vital to have a healthy sense of self-esteem—a belief in your ability to have faith, to trust, to love, and to have respect for others in a non-egotistical way. Self-esteem arises from positive thought mantras directed at making others feel good, and from affirmations that create a feeling of being comfortable with who you are.

Letting go of fear

Fear must be eliminated–fear of hurting the self's ego. Once there is no more fear, everything else that is negative will evaporate. You will no longer attract negative people or negative situations into your life because you are comfortable with what and who you are. You will not even see anyone or anything as negative, and so your personal aura will become empowered. Then you will attract loving, positive people into your world. Happiness is then well within your reach.

So use thought and word affirmations to clear away all the clutter that surrounds your ego. Accept yourself for who and what you are, throw away all that makes you scared, defensive, angry, attached, and envious—and settle comfortably into your own skin.

Using affirmation cards each day helps create positive energy.

Strengthening your personal aura

158

The empowerment of the human aura is a spiritual exercise requiring intense mental concentration and visualizations. The strength of your auric fields has much to do with your mental, emotional, and physical health. It is affected by your moods as you react to external stimuli. Those who know about auras know that there are several auric layers that surround the human body. The aura is made up of translucent colors that change, lighten, and darken according to a multitude of stimuli like the weather, the person's mood, the energy of the surrounding space, or events. Most of all, the aura is affected by physical and mental health. It is possible to empower the aura. Your aura will be strong when you have a healthy body and mind. Illness drains the aura of its intrinsic strength, and robs it of its color. Toxins in the body exhaust the aura and make it weak.

De-toxing

In recent years, many methods have been used to help the body detoxify. One way I have tried with great success is foot reflexology. I have regular sessions that help release toxins from my internal organs, which ensure I stay healthy. Reflexology works by enabling chi to flow freely throughout the body. Another way to do this is with the practice of simple chi kung exercises. As long as chi keeps moving through the body, the aura will stay strong and healthy.

I have spoken to some yogic practitioners and most of the time their humility prevents them from admitting to their siddhic powers. But I do know that they are powerful meditators and that their auras glow with a brilliance that is very divine. They tell me that it is important to lead a virtuous life to strengthen the human aura. Stay pure, they tell me. Avoid causing harm to humans, animals, and all living creatures. Try not to become intoxicated or succumb to stimulants excessively they say, and occasionally, on special days, make

Meditation and eating a healthy diet reduces internal and external stresses on the body, boosting your health and in turn your aura.

some sacrifices to purify your body. Become vegetarian, or, better yet, fast for a day. Give the mind and body a chance to release the negative things inside them. And when you chant your purification mantras, they tell me, visualize that all toxins, spiritual harm, and negative thoughts that have accumulated since beginningless time are flowing out of the openings of your body as black ink, scorpions, frogs, and snakes. Think of yourself—your body and your mind—as being completely purified.

When your consciousness is purified, your aura glows. It becomes empowered. It strengthens.

TRANSFORMING YOUR THOUGHT ENERGY

159 The "yin water bath of the seven flowers" for purification

Taking purifying baths is a popular traditional ritual, which in recent years has been effectively incorporated into the relaxation services offered in spas and detoxification centers around the world. You too can incorporate such baths in your mental and physical cleansing processes.

The yin water bath

One easy purification bath is the "yin water bath of the seven flowers." When you bathe in yin-dominated water containing the seven flowers, you set the stage for what the sages refer to as the "zenith of yin." This is achieved by immersing your entire body in water that has been activated by seven different kinds of auspicious flowers. This ritual bath encourages the bather to grow calmer and become mentally detached from his surroundings.

In this ritual, the bather focuses on each different flower, using the petals of the flowers to focus his thoughts and turn off all thoughts about anything else. This visualization helps the mind relax. It tunes into itself and slowly transcends all aspects of routine behavior. This relaxed detachment allows yang chi to rise within the person. It can be mundane yang or celestial yang. When celestial yang rises but does not get dissolved and scattered by the mind's attachment to wandering thoughts, then it makes heaven chi unite with earthly chi; the result is a luminous soaring upwards of yang energy. Then the bather truly feels centered and serene. This is regarded as magical bathing.

It is one of the best ways of making celestial yang energy rise to surround you with the essence of success. Select your flowers carefully to reflect and incorporate the colors of the five elements. Use more earth colors to strengthen relationship chi. Place greater emphasis on yellow and red flowers to strengthen the success aura. I like to recommend lots of yellow flowers, especially chrysanthemums, because they are very auspicious flowers and symbolize many good things— success, fame, and happiness. I also like white flowers like the magnolia and all the blossoms, especially the plum blossom and the cherry blossom, which signify longevity of good fortune. You can also choose jasmine, roses, and other fragrant flowers. In Bali, the spiritual island that really specializes in such baths, people like to use the frangipani, which signifies different kinds of good fortune.

Bath balls containing the essential oils of flowers that melt into the water as you bathe are a luxurious alternative to fresh blooms.

When you feel depressed, move the chi around 160

Asure fire way to strengthen your aura when you feel depressed is to move the chi in your immediate surroundings. This can be your office space if you are depressed about the state of things at the office, or your bedroom space if your depression is related to your love life, or any space where you spend much of your time.

Moving chi

Moving the chi does not involve doing anything very difficult. What is needed is for stationary objects like furniture—tables and chairs, planters and wall hangings— to be moved, shifted, or rearranged.

Vibrant color and new wall-art shifts energy and revitalizes a room.

Office chi

To move the chi in your office, get someone to help you move your desk—a few inches will be sufficient to move the chi. Anything moved more than 3 in (8 cm) will move chi. When you move a table a few inches to either the left or the right, or to the front or back, you will be setting in motion a whole series of changes in the way chi moves around you. When you move your table, you will also need to move your chair, so the flow of chi will change its pattern and set up a revitalized flow.

Wall chi

If there are photographs, posters, or paintings hanging on the wall, take them down, give them a good clean and then put them back again. Try to put them back in a slightly different place, or move them around. You might retire them and get new pictures to decorate your walls. Spend an

hour or so moving the chi. When you finish, you will be amazed at how much better you will feel. If there are planters and trees in your office, move them too. Moving plants is a very effective way to create new movements of chi. You can wind up your little session by looking around for things that should be thrown away—old pieces of paper, empty envelopes, old magazines and newspapers—so clear the clutter as well.

Bedroom chi

Remove the mattress, wash the linens, and also move the bed. Give the space under the bed a good clean-up, getting rid of the cobwebs and bad dirt that have accumulated. You will be amazed at how much stuff you have under your bed. If possible, give the mattress and pillows a good outdoor sunshine bath. Nothing lifts depression like a strong dose of yang energy.

161 When you feel weak, create sounds

When you feel weak and are convinced your life is stagnating, look for dust on your shelves and tune in to the yin chi that has obviously permeated your spaces. Yin energy can cause illness and all kinds of aches and pains that attack and assail you. You will experience an overpowering feeling of lethargy, which you simply cannot shake off.

Sometimes you do not merely feel sick, you actually become sick, succumbing to viruses and allergies. You feel that you are more vulnerable to catching diseases and physical afflictions. Simultaneously, your tolerance level retreats. It is not a nice feeling and the sooner you shake it off, the less chance it has of taking hold.

The benefits of sound therapy

There is no better cure for lethargy and weak chi in a house than sound therapy. Happy music played loud has a powerful way of sweeping away illness and weakness energy. Not all kinds of music and not all sorts of sounds are therapeutic, however. It is happy, light music that imbues an environment with strength. So play

Ringing bells and playing music shifts heavy energy and promotes and happier atmosphere.

music that engages your heart and has a happy beat, which you can dance to and sing along with. It is the same with sounds. High sounds are more uplifting than low sounds. Bells, for instance, work a lot better than drums. The sound of bells continues to resonate far beyond the time when you can hear it, and the harmonics of special clearing bells made from seven metals resonate a lot longer than ordinary ice-cream bells. When you use bells to purify any room, they leave its energy field crystal clear, instantly lifting feelings of weakness. If you are sensitive to the light spectrum of spaces, you will also feel a difference in the color spectrum of rooms, which have benefited from a sound-of-bells bath. This is because the sound of bells affects the vibrations of colors, slicing through their spectrums of light and bringing strength to the auras of colors that surround animate and inanimate objects.

Larger bells give off deeper sounds and smaller bells lighter ones. I recommend the use of smaller bells, as these create a lighter, healthier energy level in a room. If you can afford it, get a silver or golden bell in order to tap into the energy of the Moon and Sun. Even better, try to get Tibetan or Mongolian bells made from seven metals, as these offer multidimensional benefits that reflect the attributes of the seven planets. They create an aura of strength and good health. Brass bells also emit wonderful sounds, especially when some small amount of gold is added to them. When you ring bells in your living space, you will discover their sounds grow clearer with every fresh ring; walk around each room three times clockwise, and feel your spirits lift. In no time at all, you will feel energized.

TRANSFORMING YOUR THOUGHT ENERGY

When you feel unloved, bathe in a rainbow of colored lights

We all got through horrible moments of being convinced that no one cares or loves us. Even the most successful men and women are assailed by doubts about their self-worth. Moments like this descend on us for a whole variety of reasons; it is what makes the human race unique. Feelings of despondency have a range of causes.

I have discovered that trying to find root causes for such moments is of less help in dealing with them than doing something to counteract them. The most immediately revealing cure for despondency of this kind is to create a bath of rainbow-colored lights. The rainbow's seven basic colors cover an entire spectrum of cures that can be extremely healing.

Making rainbows

The easiest way to do this is to wrap a long filament light in strong rainbow-colored transparent paper. The colors on it should be red, orange, yellow, green, blue, lilac, and purple. In a darkened unlit room, turn on this specially prepared light and sit under it for about ten minutes. You then visualize the colored light beams shining down on you and entering your seated body through your crown chakra, at the top of your head. It helps if you are relaxed and calm and able to see the lights entering your head as streams of color. In your mind, differentiate between each of the colors and focus on the

A colored pendulum refracts light into rainbow colors. Each of these seven colors is associated with a particular type of healing that supports if you feel neglected.

meanings, which are listed in the box below. When you have focused on each of the individual colors, visualize all seven of them fusing into a single color—a dazzling white light. Do this by picturing the colors twirling and turning very fast until they merge into a single color. This white light is very powerful in bringing back confidence and love into your consciousness.

The Seven Benefits of the Seven Colors	
Red	For courage and strength to believe in yourself
Orange	For taking the initiative in love
Yellow	For staying grounded in all of your relationships
Green	For calm acceptance for who you are
Blue	For love and waves of caring, nurturing energy
Purple	Fo receive confidence-boosting chi
Lilac	For spiritual upliftment that convinces you that you can cope with anything.

163 Supplement your feng shui with positive expectations

Take time to focus your mind on the happiness of waking up to a new day.

You will also benefit from writing down your positive expectations.

In all the years I have practised feng shui, I have always simultaneously applied the power of positive expectations to my life. I consciously create graphic novels inside my head which star myself, always happy and smiling, and laughing with my family and close friends. In making it a life-long habit to dream of happy outcomes, I believe I have brought myself much good fortune.

Wake up to happiness

You, too, can enhance your feng shui practice with the visualisation exercise that only good news comes to you, only good people enter your life and only good results come from all your actions.

To help you get started here is a morning mental exercise that you can introduce easily into your daily life. Always allow a little time in the morning for lying in a half-asleep mode simply focussing your mind on the happiness of waking up to a brand new day, alive and well.

Focus on the positive outcomes you would like to achieve today. Whatever it is you expect of the day, make a conscious wish for it to be free of aggravations, bad news and bad incidents. Concentrate on feeling positive about what is in store for you.

Getting rid of imagined limits

Remove the barriers to success

Systematically dissolve all the blockages in your mind and supplement this exercise by also removing any physical blockages in your home to let the energy flow unencumbered around your home. Let the invisible energies flow freely without breaks and just as mental limits benefit from a breath of fresh air, likewise the energy of your home also benefits, so leave at least a couple of windows open and if possible keep some of your doors open as well. Let the outdoors come inside... unblock the blockages and you will be removing limitations from your life.

Opening doors allows chi to flow unhindered through the rooms of your home.

Those who have ever attended a lecture on positive thinking will know about setting limits. Most of the time we create breaks and hindrances to our own potential by marking out the limits of our own capabilities. This does not refer only to our perception of ability, it also encompasses the sense of worthiness. Many people simply do not believe they deserve a better life, or that they can be happier, or that they can aspire to have a better lifestyle.

Think big

Most of the time, our success is blocked by our own view of our world. In your efforts to increase your potential and enhance the results of your feng shui, do not be afraid to think big, or have big dreams. You must shrug off imagined limits to your own capabilities.

ENERGY TIP

Let chi flow through your home

Ensure that the chi can flow easily through your home by removing any awkward furniture arrangements and opening up tight corners. Open your windows to let the energy enter the house easily.

TRANSFORMING YOUR THOUGHT ENERGY

165 Tap the power within you—daily practice

To activate your good luck regularly, develop the habit of practising mental feng shui daily . Walk through the rooms of your home and around your garden. Think about what you would like to change, replace or improve. Develop a deep familiarity with the rooms of your home. This daily exercise in awareness does not take long but helps to stimulate new ideas that will allow you to enhance your home's energy.

Not many people picture their houses accurately, and are often unable to recollect every nook and cranny. Developing a habit of awareness of the space you live in is essential to improving its good fortune energy.

New awareness brings change

By increasing your awareness of your home, you are enhancing it with the vital essence of your own energy. In just a week of carrying out the daily exercise, you will see what I mean. Let your inner power guide you and, within a few months, you will have changed the appearance, the feel and the mood of all your rooms. The changes you introduce will probably be so gradual that you will be unconscious of the full effect of the transformation.

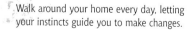
Walk around your home every day, letting your instincts guide you to make changes.

White light meditation—cocooning your home 166

Protection is a vital part of feng shui, safeguarding you and your family from misfortune, accidents and tragedies. In protective feng shui, your inner spirituality and ability to live in a state of awareness is especially powerful. A protective visualization for you or a member of your family might be of a shield or armour warding off negative, harmful energy.

Focusing your mental powers

One of the best protective visualizations for your home—and thereby you and your family—is to create a white light that cocoons your entire house and garden. This protective visualization is usually referred to as white light meditation. The protective cocoon of cosmic energy has great power.

Activating cosmic energy

Create the mental picture of white light embracing your home each night just before going to sleep. You are creating protection for everyone living in your home during the night-time yin hours.

If you make this visualization part of your night-time routine, you will strengthen your minds ability to focus. Soon it will take you less than a minute before sleeping to create your protective visual force field. You are directing cosmic energy to surround your home and keep everyone safe while they sleep.

Protect yourself and your home from nighttime yin energy by practising white light meditation.

TRANSFORMING YOUR THOUGHT ENERGY

167 Harmony of yin and yang attracts good chi

Nothing is as beneficial as having a good balance of yin and yang chi in your physical body and appearance. As well as ensuring good health, this harmonious combination of female and male chi— representing the wholeness of the "Tai Chi"—is what creates the inner serenity that others find attractive.

Harmonize your body and mind

Harmonizing yin and yang in your life often means striking a good balance in all the things you do, as well as in your surroundings. Think of opposite characteristics: softness and toughness, coolness and warmth, quiet and noise, dark and light. Keeping a balance is not as difficult as it sounds. All that is needed is a conscious effort not to go to any extreme in the way you live. Good feng shui living encourages moderation in everything you do.

Find life's rhythm

When your body is not excessively taxed in any way, it is able to rejuvenate itself. Similarly, do not allow your mental powers to become exhausted by making too many demands of yourself—or allowing others to do so. The same is true of your

The ancient symbol of yin and yang clearly represents two opposites working together while remaining individual.

Aim to create a good balance in your life, as this will give you inner tranquillity.

emotional energy. Make sure your daily timetable includes appropriate amounts of rest time and work time without too much of either.

With this kind of harmony, you will never feel too tired or aggravated. Your life will flow at a pace that creates a relaxed inner calmness that others will find restful and attractive.

An auspicious face reflects inner vibrancy

No face, no matter how beautiful or well balanced the features, can be charismatic or auspicious if it does not reflect the vibrant personality within. Charisma is not about having perfect features, a fine complexion or a good figure. It is not the packaging that creates charisma, but the projection of the personality. If your personality radiates yang chi then your aura will give you a presence in any room that will attract people to you.

Developing charisma

To bring out your powerful personal charisma, start by creating brightness and lightness within yourself. You must think powerful to become powerful, and love the uniqueness of your own appearance to be beautiful. Perhaps most important of all, believe that your whole personality has a resounding vibrancy that gives you a presence.

This belief in yourself does not come overnight, but is built up over time. The sooner you make a start, the sooner your inner charisma will begin shining through. Often the inner vibrancy you are seeking to develop is enhanced by the belief that you look good. In this way there is a simultaneous boost to the radiancy of your inner self and outer self. The more one is enhanced, the more the other benefits, and vice versa.

ENERGY TIP

Begin creating an auspicious face by always looking your best

Paying attention to your physical wellbeing and personal grooming is an ideal way to start creating your auspicious face. The very act of making an extra effort with your physical appearance, perhaps using make-up to give you a healthy glow, will give your confidence the kind of boost that jump-starts personal charisma.

Taking care of your appearance encourages a sense of wellbeing from which charisma can grow.

169 Five important features of your face

In Chinese culture, your face is said to be a mirror to your soul. It often reveals a lot more about yourself than you want, which is why masks have such an important place in Chinese tradition. In old China, officials at court learned early on to hide their feelings, their moods, and their attitudes. They consciously worked on not allowing what was in their hearts and souls to show on their faces. Many of the secrets of the "hidden face" are now lost, although references to them continue to color the metaphors of local dialects of the Chinese language.

Mystery creates charisma

Today, we use cosmetics to define our features, drawing attention to our eyes and mouths. We use foundation cream to make our skins look as flawless as possible, evening out our complexions. Making up our faces is the modern equivalent of creating a mask—though the effects are more subtle.

Let your face look groomed and beautiful. If you choose to use cosmetics to improve your appearance, you can look on make-up as a mask that conceals your inner self, or as a way to emphasize the best in you. For example, a colorful shade of lipstick enhances the positive effect of a smiling or laughing mouth.

ENERGY TIP

What gives your appearance personality?

The forehead, cheeks, eyes, nose and mouth are the five most important defining features that give flesh and substance to your overall appearance.

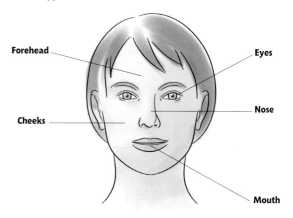

Remember that you are in control of the persona you are creating. Make up is the first step towards projecting your personality while not revealing everything about yourself. Mystery is a vital ingredient of charisma.

Know your own face

Just as it is important to develop an awareness of the rooms in your home, it is beneficial to know your own face well. This is not as easy as it sounds—other people see your different expressions but you only see yourself reflected in a mirror. However, make the effort to discover the colors that suit you and how to enhance your features.

Chinese masks focus on the five features that give vibrancy to a face.

A clear complexion attracts harmony and luck   170

protect your face from damaging ultra-violet rays. Some sunlight, however, is vital for invigorating yang energy—think of the uplifting effect of looking at the first rays of sunlight in the morning. Your face benefits from Moon energy. This is echoed by pearlescent powders, which add sheen and clarity to your face. The Chinese prefer the face to resemble the Moon rather than the Sun, hence the preference for pale rather than suntanned faces.

A pale face reflects moonlight, which is auspicious and preferable to a tanned face.

The first step to a flawless complexion is to keep your skin clean and well moisturized.

According to the Chinese a smooth complexion is the most important ingredient of a lucky face. So today's breakthroughs in facial creams are a real boon for those wanting to create a charismatic and successful face. Always make sure you clean your face regularly each night before going to bed.

Mixing yin and yang

The secret to an auspicious face is the right mix of yin and yang chi. Too much yang sunlight causes the face to crease and become rough, so it is a good idea to reduce the direct impact of sunlight. Wear a large, shading sun hat and a sun cream to

TRANSFORMING YOUR THOUGHT ENERGY

171 Bright eyes and a steady gaze brings good chi

Your eyes reveal so much about you: your health, your mood, your character, and your emotions. They are the windows to what is in your heart. People discover so much about you just by looking into your eyes. Every morning, as you prepare for the day, pay attention to how your eyes will appear to others. If you want to create an impression of vitality and intelligence, it is vital that your eyes sparkle.

Inauspicious tired eyes

Tired, dry, or red eyes reflect a listlessness or instability of energy within our minds and bodies. Often they are the first indications of excessive "heat" in the body. Whatever the cause, tired eyes are never auspicious, so there is no need even to mention bloodshot eyes! Tired eyes have a dullness to them that is very uninspiring. They are usually an indication that you need plenty of sleep or some restful yin chi. If you make a conscious effort to light up your eyes, treating them for redness or dryness, and making sure that you get enough sleep, they will enhance your personal charisma.

Let your eyes speak

Bright eyes are a magnet, attracting helpful people who bring plenty of good chi and wonderful opportunities. You can also use eye make-up to define your eyes and add luster to your eyelids.

A feng shui tip is to develop the strength of your eyes so that you can keep them open without flickering. Steady eyes that have the ability to gaze straight without blinking reflect a calm personality. Some people have even developed their eye strength to make their eyes powerfully piercing, but there is no need to go that far.

Don't forget to keep a slight smile in your eyes. If you do not, you risk them looking unfriendly or, worse, hostile. Remember, good chi comes to those whose demeanour is unthreatening. Develop a steady gaze that is friendly and inviting, and meet other people's eyes in an open manner.

Project a charismatic personality by always keeping eye contact with colleagues and friends alike.

Activate your third eye to expand your world   172

People are now becoming familiar with the third eye, which lies just beneath the skin's surface between the eyebrows. The third eye is our mystical eye, which sees all the spiritual and psychic aspects of our worlds that our regular two eyes cannot see.

Open your mind
To activate your third eye, focus your concentration on the area between your eyebrows. Rub this part of your face in the morning when you wake up and at night just before you go to sleep. After you have done this regularly for about a month you will start to become increasingly aware of images that flash through your mind. At first you will hardly notice them, or they will not seem significant, but over time they will weave unexpected messages and stories into your consciousness. By opening your third eye, you will become more aware of space and time, and this will help you slowly but surely to live a fuller and more meaningful life.

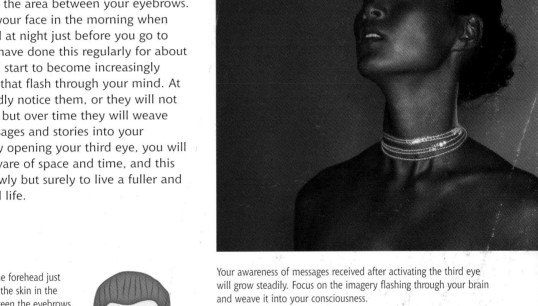

Your awareness of messages received after activating the third eye will grow steadily. Focus on the imagery flashing through your brain and weave it into your consciousness.

The third eye lies on the forehead just beneath the surface of the skin in the centre of the face between the eyebrows.

Activate the power of the third eye by gently rubbing around it in a circular motion every morning and evening.

Discover your psychic abilities
For some people rubbing the third eye also creates pathways into their inner instincts. Some people call this a psychic ability but this is not the monopoly of a chosen few—all of us have it—but sadly not many people have the confidence to trust their instincts sufficiently. When you activate your third eye, think yourself into a state of readiness for your own psychic abilities to emerge gradually.

173 Discover your miraculous breath

If you want to develop a "presence"—the kind of charisma that brings you attention the moment you walk into a room—make a conscious effort to develop deep breathing. The miraculous breath governs the quality of chi energy that surrounds you, so the ability to breathe strongly and steadily without any seeming effort is a powerful key to good health and an aura of positive yang chi.

Discover extra strength and vigour

All Chinese martial arts and chi kung exercises are based on focussed breathing. This is because breathing shapes our effectiveness in all our activities. Start paying attention to your breath—most people's breathing is too shallow. At night consciously take deep breaths to sleep more soundly. When you awake, you will find that you really are more refreshed.

It is the same during your working hours. When you make a real effort to breathe more deeply something magical happens to your energy levels. Charismatic people always breathe deeply and steadily: they are rarely out of breath nor are they easily tired out.

The movements of tai chi are based around the steadiness and control of one's breathing.

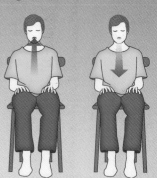

ENERGY TIP

Practicing deep breathing

Start discovering your magical breath by practicing steady and deep breathing on a daily basis. Simply sit upright in a chair with your hands resting on your knees and concentrate on letting the air flow in and out of your lungs. Do this exercise until deep breathing becomes second nature, re-energizing your life and, by extension, your home.

Practice important morning rituals

174

Look upon the morning as a beautiful and auspicious beginning to an active, fulfilled and meaningful day. Try to capture the Hour of the Dragon (from 7am to 9am) when the morning's majestic yang energy is at full strength. If you sleep through this time, you are letting this revitalizing energy go to waste. Try to be up and about so you can enjoy the special, invigorating morning air.

Enjoy the cool of the day

Early morning is the time when yang energy is young. The sun's rays are gentle, and the heat of the day has not yet become oppressive because the cool of the night still lingers. This is the best time to perform all your important morning rituals—some people workout, some do tai chi or yoga, while others meditate.

Stay centered and beautiful

These morning rituals help keep you centred to the cosmic energy of the Universe. For example, you might start the day with a refreshing wash before meditating in the early morning rays of the sun. Meditating, you can feel your own purity and beauty in the presence of the divine, as uplifting yang energy enters your body and gives a wonderful boost to start your day.

Early morning meditation during the Hour of the Dragon encourages yang energy to enter your mind and body. This gives you mental and spiritual vitality that will keep you energized throughout the day.

ENERGY TIP

Early morning meditation

Before meditating it is helpful to have a bath or shower, then wear some of your precious jewellery, even some sparkling "bling". Contrary to popular belief, it is not best to meditate wearing loose clothes or to be devoid of all make-up and jewels. Try the following meditation to get your day off to an excellent start: close your eyes lightly and let your mind transport you to the Garden of Eden. Here, imagine yourself meeting with beautiful Goddesses and magical Dakinis. Let their goodness, purity and divinity enter your soul and energize your being.

TRANSFORMING YOUR THOUGHT ENERGY

175 Verbalize all your triumphant moments—rejoice!

Give yourself permission to think and talk about times when particular aspects of your life are going well—perhaps when you achieve a goal or complete a project and feel like rejoicing. Don't be afraid to give yourself a regular pat on the back. Likewise, notice the achievements of those who are near and dear to you, and celebrate their successes with them. The power of rejoicing in all our worthwhile achievements—as well as those of other people—is a powerful catalyst to greater success in the future.

Nurture your success
Think of each small triumph as a seed for even greater success in future. Your achievements will multiply and develop in your life if they are well nurtured. Rejoicing as you achieve each and every one of your goals creates the right conditions for future success.

By extending this celebratory feeling towards others—friends, colleagues and work mates—you will also prevent feelings of envy or jealousy from arising. In this way, you guard against attracting negative chi.

If you remember to rejoice in the positive aspects of your life often enough you will succeed in creating an aura of joyousness around you, untainted by any hostile or negative emotions.

Chapter Four

Special Techniques
For Success

Now learn how to fire up your finances, your career and your relationships with a series of special energy rituals, Each will boost your personal success, thereby enhancing your charisma and your inner strength.

Discover how some plum blossom can generate the chi that will help you find luck in love, how symbols ca draw in prosperity and how personal exercises can ensure that wishes are fulfilled. Improving your personal finances can be achieved simply by growing a plant in an auspicious area of the house while utilizing the power of water will be enough to cause a change for the better in your career luck. Invoking the strength of symbols and holy objects can also attract the good energy that will turn your luck around.

Enjoy feeling your life improve as each tip will give an extra boost to your home life, bank balance and career.

176 Jump-starting a stagnant life

Use the eight aspirations formula of the Pa Kua to place feng shui symbols of good fortune in the different compass corners of the home. This is a simple yet effective formula in which each of the eight directions stands for a different desired goal.

Stimulating relationships luck

If you want to fire up your relationships luck, bringing romance and love luck into your life, ensure that the southwest corner of your home is washed with bright lights to create fire energy. This, in turn, produces the earth element that brings nesting luck. Any symbol made of crystals—such as mandarin ducks and double happiness symbols of love—will jazz up your relationships luck tremendously.

Activating career luck

If your life is stagnating due to lack of challenges, activate the north corner of your living room, or work area, with a water feature. A small aquarium will generate yang energy if you keep a few little fish that are active swimmers. This will make you upwardly mobile, bringing new opportunities and challenges into your work life. Energy from an aquarium is especially beneficial if you are developing a career in a big company.

Generating recognition luck

Stagnation can also be caused by the constant disappointment of lack of success or not receiving positive feedback. If you want your work to be appreciated, and to gain recognition and praise, jump-start your creativity by bringing in the kind of chi that fosters encouragement and support into your life. Achieve this by placing lots of plants in the south. This stimulates the energy of the wood element, producing vital fire element energy. When you generate this kind of elemental flow in the south of your rooms, it activates your recognition luck, bringing you more attention.

Placing a crystal geode in the northwest of your home brings you mentor luck, and the support of an influential mentor will create new opportunities in your life.

Attracting mentor luck

Finally, if you want to meet influential people who can open the right doors to new pathways in your life, jump-start your mentor luck. Nothing makes the adrenaline flow faster than having a worthwhile mentor "adopt" you as a protégé, giving you the support and encouragement you need to achieve your goals. Attract this kind of luck by placing a large piece of crystal geode in the northwest of your home. The crystal geode exudes much-needed metal energy, bringing the mentor luck that will make all the difference to your life.

Place a water feature in the southwest

177

Wealth luck opens new possibilities and the power to liberate yourself from the bondage of a staid routine. In the years up to 2024, you can activate the powerful wealth-bringing potential of the Period of Eight (see Tip 74). Its indirect spirit resides in the southwest corner of the home, so placing a water feature here will be incredibly beneficial for your wealth luck. This is also an excellent way of keeping the feng shui of your home up-to-date for the current period.

Digging a pond in the garden

To attract serious wealth into your life, the water feature you choose should be of substantial size— a pool or fishpond dug into the ground in the southwest of your garden, for example, is ideal. Make sure that the water is visible from inside your home, and keep it clean at all times. Of course, whether you decide to activate the southwest area of your garden in this way will depend upon the space you have available to you. Although digging a pond is a major task, the rewards will be worthwhile and you will soon reap the benefits.

A bubbling fountain, or pond in which the water is constantly stirred by the movements of fish, will energize a southwest corner with yang chi, attracting wealth luck to your home.

Adding a water feature in a flat

If you live in a flat, a small water feature might be your only realistic option, so make the most of it. Choose a design, such as a six-tier waterfall, that showcases the movement of water. With clever use of lighting, you can keep the water glittering and sparkling as it flows. It is also important that the water is clean and keeps moving. This will create the yang energy needed to increase your wealth luck.

178 Allowing yang energy into the facing palace of your home

The facing palace is the part of the house where chi enters. It is always the space just inside the front door, often referred to as the hall or foyer. Keeping the main door opposite the facing palace open as much as possible allows a steady stream of revitalizing yang energy to enter the house. Of course you need to consider security but, if you have a fence around your property, you might be able to keep the door into the house open—particularly if you have a dog that will bark at strangers. Feng shui celestial protectors, such as a pair of Fu dogs, will also guard the home from any harmful energy entering via the main door.

A well-lit, spacious and clutter-free facing palace attracts beneficial chi into your home.

Keeping halls clear of clutter
This facing palace must be kept clutter-free so that energy remains auspicious. Good energy here will flow into the rest of the house so long as it is not impeded. Never keep shoes or slippers here as this symbolizes the kicking out of the good chi coming in. Instead, keep your shoes inside a cupboard and hang the coats of visiting friends elsewhere, too.

Never allow old newspapers and magazines to pile up near the door to the facing palace. This kind of blockage will cause obstacles to manifest suddenly in your work and personal life. You might find, for example, that agreed-upon contracts suffer unexpected setbacks and that previously sound relationships turn bad. A clutter-free, airy, brightly lit facing palace, however, allows chi to gather before entering your home, enhancing good fortune in all aspects of your life.

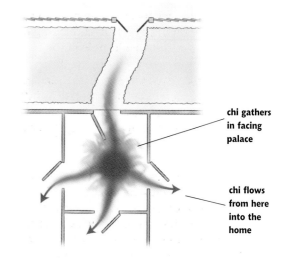

chi gathers in facing palace

chi flows from here into the home

Place a painting of 100 birds just outside your front door

This wonderful tip has benefited so many people since I first suggested it that I am continuing to advise my readers to follow it. In feng shui, winged creatures symbolize a variety of opportunities that have the potential to change one's life for the better. Birds—especially birds with colourful plumage—not only bring good news into the home, but open your eyes to new creative ideas.

If you have serious ambitions to build and own your own business, look for a painting of a hundred birds, a thousand birds, even a million birds—the more the better. If you can find a painting of a million birds—most will then be mere dots in the sky—and it appeals to you, invite it into your home as it is sure to bring you good luck. In New York there is a famous art

Pictures of birds bring good fortune—the more birds the better and it does not matter what type they are, although colorful plumage is particularly auspicious.

gallery that sells the work of a well-known Singaporean artist who paints nothing but millions of birds. His works sell for millions of dollars and he has become rich just by selling his million-birds paintings.

Birds are always auspicious

All kinds of birds can feature in your painting and bring you good luck. There is no such thing as a bird that brings bad news. Even crows—said to be messengers of the all-powerful, compassionate but wrathful gods—and owls, symbols of wisdom, have positive connotations despite some people believing that they bring bad luck.

180 Energizing a room with the Sun and Moon sign

The signs of the Sun and the Moon have an empowering energy, particularly when combined. The New Moon is perceived as a crescent shape and the Sun is visualized as a full circle. Together they form the Sun and Moon sign which, over time, has evolved into the Chinese gold ingot. The New Moon forms the base, with its ends tilted upwards, and the Sun appears above it.

Yin and yang balance

The Sun and Moon sign has several auspicious connotations. Firstly, it signifies the balance of yin and yang, with the Moon being yin and the Sun being yang. The sign also represents night and day when moonlight and sunlight wash the Earth in turn with light.

Moonlight brings serenity, enabling people to rebuild their strength and stamina even as they rest, while sunlight brings life, harvest and prosperity. One cannot exist without the other. If you have no time to rest the body and rejuvenate, your mind and spirit will not be able to make the most of the Sun's light and energy. Together the Sun and the Moon are a powerful energizing force.

An auspiciously placed mirror in the shape of the Sun will reflect yang energy into your home.

The shapes of Chinese gold ingots are based on the Sun and Moon signs.

Activating the power of the signs

As Chinese gold ingots not only signify the Sun and the Moon but are also a symbol of wealth and prosperity, they are a wonderful symbol of good luck when placed in your home.

Another way to bring the illuminating energy of the Sun and the Moon into your home is to hang a drawing or an embroidery of the signs in your living room. Reflect on the power of the signs to activate their energy.

Wear mantra gold jewelry to attract beneficial chi

There are many beautiful mantras that can be worn as gold jewellery. Fashioning a mantra in gold is a wonderful way to invoke the power of these holy syllables and sounds, activating a special, divine energy.

The wearing of sacred mantras as adornments is not so much feng shui as inspired by feng shui. I discovered that the traditions of Tibetan Buddhism include many rituals that appear similar to those of feng shui except that Buddhism uses many spiritual syllables and symbols to attract good fortune or to protect against misfortune.

I have been studying and researching Tibetan Buddhist rituals now for ten years, and have discovered many wonderful symbols, mantras and rituals of protection and luck enhancement. Wearing mantra gold jewellery is one of the most popular ways to safeguard against misfortune, spirit harm and other kinds of bad luck.

Popular mantras

Of the many mantras fashioned into pendants, bracelets and rings perhaps the most widely worn continue to be those that carry the most popular mantras, that of Tara, Mother of all the Buddhas:

OM TARE TUTTARE TURE SOHA

meaning "may the meaning of the mantra take hold in my mind" and the mantra of the Compassionate Buddha:

OM MANI PADME HUMA

All the teachings of the Buddha are contained in this mantra, which cannot be translated into a simple phrase. It invokes benevolence and empathy for all living things.

In addition you can also look for powerful seed syllables such as OM or HUM that are made from gold and fashioned into

Wearing gold mantra jewellery and visualizing its powerful positive energy is a wonderful way to enhance your spirituality and ward off bad luck.

pendants. These pendants may take on the guise of personal adornment but they are really centres of powerful protective energy. When you wear them, visualize rays of blessing light emanating from them. This kind of visualization activates their power tremendously. If you feel in any kind of danger, or have any sort of premonition, rub the pendant and recite the mantra. You will find that your fears subside instantly, leaving you feeling a lot calmer.

182 Firing up your love life with plum blossom luck

Creating plum blossom luck is an effective way to bring in marriage opportunities. Placing one or more of the traditional symbols of love—a pair of birds, the double happiness sign, the dragon, and the phoenix—in the southwest corner of your home is all you need to do to activate it.

Finding a suitable mate
Plum blossom luck can work for or against you, however. At best, the person you attract will be someone good natured and dependable who will make you happy throughout your life. You need to beware, though, of attracting the opposite—a person who is not suitable for you, and who will cause you heartache and problems. It is not enough to create the energy of marriage, you need to take steps to attract a good mate. For this, you must add peach blossom luck.

Activating peach blossom luck
For peach blossom luck, first identify your personal peach blossom animal. This will be either the Horse, the Rooster, the Rabbit, or the Rat. In feng shui, only these four animals of the cardinal signs are counted as peach blossom animals. Place the animal's symbol in a prominent place in its corresponding part of your home—the Rat is located in the north, the Horse in the south, the Rabbit in the east, and the Rooster in the west.

Secondly, identify the peach blossom location for this year or the coming one. In 2008 it is in the northeast, in the south in 2009 and in the north in 2010. Activate the sector with a symbol of your

Plum blossom luck energizes your love life with new possibilities. Beware, though, that the potential mates it attracts may be good or bad for you.

peach blossom animal. Unless yours is the Rooster, this will necessitate finding more than one peach blossom animal symbol for both auspicious locations in your home.

ENERGY TIP

Your peach blossom animal

Your peach blossom animal is governed by your Chinese Zodiac sign. If you were born in the year of the Rooster, the Snake, or the Ox, your peach blossom animal is the Horse; for the Dragon, the Rat, or the Monkey, it is the Rooster; for the Rabbit, the Sheep, or the Boar, it is the Rat; and for the Tiger, the Horse, or the Dog, it is the Rabbit.

Dragon and phoenix vases for peace and harmony

183

Vases this shape and color—ox-blood red—are excellent feng shui. The golden dragon and phoenix image symbolize a happy marriage blessed with prosperity.

Investing in a golden dragon or phoenix vase is regarded as one of the most satisfying ways to create a calm, happy, and prosperous home. For centuries, Chinese royalty decorated their palaces and homes with vases. There would not be a single room that did not have pairs of vases created from porcelain and cloisonné, and decorated with different types of auspicious symbols.

In the outer, more public rooms, gigantic vases decorated in brilliant hues and featuring various longevity and prosperity symbols would be used to flank entrances and doorways, while deeper into the inner quarters of the home, vases made of gold, cloisonné, and special porcelain would be used to highlight important corners.

Wealth vases

In yet more private inner sanctums, families would have at least one wealth vase. This would be passed down from generation to generation and its presence in the home would ensure the steady accumulation of wealth within the family. Wealth vases are filled and consecrated with special substances that symbolize family assets and wealth, such as real gold and precious stones. In addition, wealth vases would also contain soil from the property of a wealthy person and, if possible, cash from a wealthy person, in the form of a few coins. Symbolically, this effectively borrows his or her wealth chi and activates the wealth vase.

Vases are considered to be one of the eight precious objects in Chinese Buddhism, although as a symbolic presence in the home its popularity goes beyond the boundaries of religious or spiritual significance. In Chinese the word "vase" is ping, which also sounds like "peace."

The image of the phoenix always symbolizes wonderful opportunities coming your way. By itself, the phoenix is a powerful symbol, attracting a sudden surge of good fortune. The phoenix is also the king of the birds, and bird energy always brings good news.

184 Invoking the four protector-guardians for your home

There are four symbolic guardians that the Chinese are extremely fond of putting inside their homes. They are known as the four Heavenly Kings in Chinese legends, and as the four Dharma Protectors in Tibetan Buddhist stories. These guardians absorb the temptations and harm from spirits that come from the four directions. So, having them in your home keeps away damage caused by spirits and entities from other dimensions that cause illness, accidents, and injury to residents.

How the four protectors help
The four heavenly guardians protect us from the harm we may inflict upon ourselves, which is usually the result of our non-virtuous actions such as killing, stealing, and acting dishonorably or in an evil manner. This is why they are referred to as dharma protectors. They protect us from the evil and negative parts of ourselves. These four guardians hold a symbolic tool unique to their activities, and they each take charge of a different compass direction.

Shown here are (from left): Mo Li Ching, guardian of the East; Mo Li Hai, who protects the West; Mo Li Hung, guardian of the South; and Mo Li Shou, guardian of the North.

The guardian of the East is Mo Li Chung. He holds a magic sword with the words "earth, water, fire, and wind" on its blade. His sword is metal, to overcome wood chi moving from the East. He should be placed facing East.

The guardian of the West is Mo Li Hai. He holds a four-string mandolin, which, when played, causes great balls of fire to fall from heaven, thus destroying the metal energy of the West. He should be placed facing West.

The guardian of the South is Mo Li Hung, who carries a magic umbrella. When open, it creates total darkness, putting out the fire energy of the South. It can also unleash tidal waves and earthquakes that can destroy all negative forces. He should face South.

The guardian of the North is Mo Li Shou. He carries a pearl in one hand and a serpent in the other. Sometimes, he is shown seated on an elephant. He should face North in order to overcome the bad energy coming from there.

Creating a home altar to open pathways into spirituality

185

It does not matter what faith you follow, but if you want to open pathways to growth in awareness of all things spiritual, you might wish to consider setting up a small altar in your home. Altars are expressions of spiritual aspirations, and the best kind of altars are those dedicated to the God presence with which we each are most familiar and comfortable. I am one of those who believes that God is a word that signifies and personifies the highest good in all of us.

I have many altars in my home and they create a wonderful spiritual river of energy that is really very beautiful. When unhappiness arises in the house, it evaporates pretty quickly. When there is anger, it also dissipates in no time at all, and when those of us in the house suffer from fear, dissatisfaction, or frustration, something always happens to distract us from our negative emotions.

My altars are rather elaborate, with plenty of the five offering objects that are usually associated with altars: flowers, water, food, incense, and lights. I have been taught to replace these offerings daily in order to invoke the spiritual presence of cosmic forces that bless my home and engender within us all the desire to live virtuous lives and be beneficial to others. Virtue in this instance does not mean being goody-two-shoes, but rather that we observe the basic tenets of not harming others and not doing anything in excess.

You can set up your altar according to what works for you. I have often been asked if altars need to be consecrated, and I would say preferably so. But, here again, it is up to you really. What I am advocating is the notion that, by inviting the God presence into your home, you create a spiritual energy that can only do you good.

Altars do not have to be traditional; exhibiting eclectic items you love is still effective.

186 Magnifying sacred energy with holy objects

If you purchase sacred art, always find out about its history and the way it should be displayed.

Treating holy objects with respect
Spiritual energy is something truly hard to explain. It must be felt and experienced. I always advise people I know that they should be very discerning when inviting holy objects into their homes. Precisely because they are sacred images, it is best to bring in only those that have a meaning for you. Do not bring in strange-looking images with which you are totally unfamiliar—you must be able to recognize images of gods and deities you display. If they come from a country you are unfamiliar with, it is always a good idea to ask how they should be exhibited and whether there may be any taboos associated with showing them.

I almost always feel a jolt when I see Buddha heads in people's homes. Although I am sure no disrespect is meant by people who display Buddha heads in their homes, nevertheless I feel a great sadness when I realize that these antique sacred objects may have been plundered from holy grounds and temples. I have also seen Kuan Yin images as lamp stands and table stands; I cringe at this disrespectful display of what to many millions of people are devotional statues. The general rule is to treat all sacred objects with the utmost respect. If you invite them into your home, place at least one offering in front of them, even if it is just a light that shines on their beauty. This way, you do not think of them as decorations, but rather as adding to the spiritual chi of the home.

If you want your living space to be sacred, then having holy objects inside your home is certain to help you achieve this quickly and efficiently. Holy objects work as powerful symbols that communicate with us at higher dimensions of consciousness. These may be religious paintings and images or statues of deities. Each of the major religious traditions has truly stunning images, paintings, and works of art that can be exhibited in the home, given a respectable and prominent display space, and, if we so wish, even consecrated.

When you invite religious objects of any faith into your home, you are creating spiritual energy within it. Holy objects magnify spiritual chi just by being there. This is why so many Chinese have the image of Kuan Yin—the Goddess of Mercy or Compassion—in their homes. To many Chinese, Kuan Yin is the ultimate sacred object. They feel that her mere presence in a home imbues it with her blessings.

Display the eight precious treasures in your home 187

The eight precious treasures symbolize prosperity, wealth, and abundance, which are manifested in eight different ways. The presence of all eight precious treasures creates a powerful spiritual ambience when you mentally offer these treasures and dedicate the good luck they bring to the highest good.

These precious treasures feature prominently in the Mandala offerings which Buddhists create in their minds as part of their daily meditation practice. These are, therefore, very powerful and important symbols, whose presence in the home adds tremendously to the creation of a calm spiritual presence within it.

These precious treasures are:

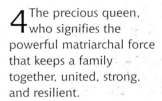

1 The precious vase, which signifies peace and serenity in a household. It is also the wealth vase, which symbolically refers to a family's wealth and assets. When you protect the vase and treat it with care, you are safeguarding your assets and also watching them multiply.

2 The precious wheel, which signifies the attainment of knowledge and the achievement of the highest scholastic honors.

3 The precious jewel, which signifies wealth in its most beautiful forms as treasures of the earth: gold, diamonds, and precious stones.

4 The precious queen, who signifies the powerful matriarchal force that keeps a family together, united, strong, and resilient.

5 The precious general, who signifies good security and protection for the home and its residents.

6 The precious minister, who takes care of all administrative matters and ensures that life flows smoothly and well.

7 The precious horse, which brings recognition and fame to the household and ensures the spread of your good name.

8 The precious elephant, which brings an abundance of male heirs into a house–a true personification of descendants' luck.

188 A rosewood Ru Yi strengthens the breadwinner's chi

In the old days, men of power and authority in China carried a scepter called the Ru Yi—often made of jade, carved with auspicious objects or fashioned in gold, and studded with precious gemstones. Even the emperor carried this symbol of imperial authority and royal power—said effectively to transmit the authority and power of his lifeforce. Since then, the Ru Yi has been revered as a symbol of high authority.

Today, placing the Ru Yi in your home and office is believed to confer the chi of leadership and influence. If you are a manager, or work in a supervisory capacity, the Ru Yi will ensure that your authority is acknowledged and that your judgments are respected. It is the best feng shui tool for managers and executives. Placed in the home, it is an amazingly effective tool for the breadwinner.

Ru Yi etiquette
It is, however, important to ensure that you get a Ru Yi that is in keeping with your status so never place a Ru Yi in your home or office that is plastic, or display one that is made of some cheap metal. You simply must look for a Ru Yi that suggests some real substance. The size is not as important

The mystic knot is a good fortune symbol often found on the Ru Yi.

as the way the Ru Yi has been crafted. Remember that the Ru Yi represents the power of the high official who has the authority to make important decisions. So you need a Ru Yi that symbolizes this power. Only then will it confer powerful authority luck for those who want this type of influence.

When the Ru Yi is also embellished with other symbols of good fortune, such as the mystical knot or the 8 Immortals—manifesting eight types of good fortune associated with longevity, good health, happiness, success, and prosperity—it has added significance. Each of the Immortals signifies the attainment of the highest levels of success in different professions. Place the Ru Yi in your study at home in the Northwest direction.

A hand-carved rosewood Ru Yi is excellent for someone who is climbing the corporate career ladder. Rosewood is an auspicious wood in feng shui, and wood also symbolizes growth chi,

Exhibiting spiritual friends from other realms   189

Some of you reading this may already be aware that we all have spiritual friends, spirit guides, and astral companions from other realms. When we cleanse our space and invite in spiritual chi, we are also opening doorways into other realms and dimensions of existence.

Those among us who are fortunate enough to have been shown a window into this invisible world know that this awareness is something that can be developed, expanded, and speeded up. So many people are now coming forward with accounts of their experiences of other realms of existence, where they speak with beings, birds, and animals, that I am now convinced we have many friends from other dimensions—many more than we know!

Coincidences and messages

In order to open the window into those worlds a little wider, you may want to consciously tune in to clues and coincidences when they happen. Become sensitive to messages from the cosmic realms. For instance, if you keep seeing a certain plant, or coming into contact with a certain animal, you may construe this as a message cutting across realms. Messages come in the books that make their way to you (even this one), in the images that come on the moment you turn on the television, the first thing you see on the road when going to work, the object of a conversation over the phone, on the bus, at work. It is the recurring themes to which you should pay attention. String these coincidences together and see whether a message is, indeed, coming to you.

Finding Spiritual Friends

Many people have affinities with certain animals, particular flowers, or a type of bird or fish. These could be your friends from another realm. The next time you attend an art show, see if anything grabs you. Note whether anything is irresistible to you. Images that tug and pull at your heart-strings always mean something.

When I first set eyes on a colorful Tibetan thangka painting, I literally drooled; I could not take my eyes off its striking images. Later, when I visited Nepal, I made my way to a thangka shop and spent two magical days going crazy over these paintings. Today my home is filled with many beautiful thangka paintings of different buddhas. Of course I love to think of these buddhas as my friends, reaching out for me through time and space and continuing to teach me as I live out this existence. Whatever they are or may be, following my instincts on this has led to a quantum leap in my spiritual consciousness.

190 Create an aquarium filled with little fish for career luck

It is possible to benefit from the positive chi of swimming fish no matter the size of your room. The curving sides of a large aquarium and small goldfish bowl denote a smooth, constant path to wellbeing and prosperity.

To boost your career luck, activate a north corner in your home. Locate the north corner of a room where you spend much of your time then place an aquarium here. The strong swimming action of small fish provides a constant source of yang energy. If you have a large enough aquarium, you can further enhance good chi by having fish in multiples of nine.

Keeping healthy fish is good chi

Aquariums are excellent as feng shui activators so long as they are properly maintained. Keep the aquarium well aerated so that the water does not become stagnant and the fish have a plentiful supply of oxygen. If the fish start dying, the water quality is probably not good enough. However, if one or two die for no apparent reason it is possible that they have absorbed your bad luck.

Enhance lucky corners with auspicious objects 191

The Chinese are great believers in the power of symbolic feng shui. Deities, divine celestial creatures, heavenly symbols, trees, flowers, and all kinds of shapes and colours possess a variety of auspicious meanings. In practice, inspiration is taken from the I Ching (the Book of Changes) where symbols of broken and unbroken lines have powerful connotations. Knowledge of the meaning of these symbols, and their relationship with the five elements, provides enlightenment for the practice of symbolic feng shui.

Locating lucky corners
Symbolic objects have most power when they are placed in the lucky corners of your home. Each year different parts of your home become auspicious. Keep yourself up to date with where lucky corners are, using a compass to locate them. This allows you to increase your fortune chi for the year.

Activating different energies
Selecting auspicious objects for lucky corners can be confusing due to a number of feng shui formulas recommending a variety of elements and objects for different corners. However, it is perfectly good practice to place multiple objects in any corner to enhance different dimensions of luck. In 2011, for instance, the Northwest, the corner affecting the luck of the Patriarch, is very auspicious as the number 8 has flown to the NW sector in the annual chart. This is a metal sector and placing anything made of metal here would be auspicious for the father of the family. Another way to activate this sector would be with the use of earth energy ie things made of crystal, as earth produces metal in the 5-element cycle. According to the 8 Aspirations formula, the NW is also the part of the house that attracts mentoring luck to residents, so placing a picture of an older father figure here is excellent. This demonstrates the many ways you can activate any sector. Note that the luckiest sectors of your house will change from year to year. In 2012 the luckiest sector is the West and in 2013 it will be in the Northeast.

A pair of brass Chi lin is not only auspicious but a safeguard against bad luck befalling the household.

A pair of mandarin ducks placed in the Southwest sector activate love and good relationship luck.

Creative thinking
Be imaginative in fine-tuning the different aspects of your feng shui practice to activate all the auspicious corners of your home without overwhelming it with too many symbolic objects. To gain the most beneficial energy you might, for example, place water in the east corner of your garden, or position a gold wu lou in the east corner of your bedroom.

192 Place Horse images in the south to gain recognition

Inviting images of the horse into your home simultaneously invites in the star of the nobleman. While the horse brings recognition and promotion, the nobleman brings prosperity. Add images of the horse to the south corner of your home to bring in extremely beneficial energy. The Horse is auspicious in the south in all years, so it's always good feng shui to have a Horse in this location—although it is a good idea to change your Horse figurine from time to time to update the energy.

Images of the horse are always best placed in the south corner of your home.

For those born in the years of the Rooster, Snake and Ox, the Horse is a peach blossom luck animal. This means that having a Horse in the south—especially during a year in which the Horse enjoys good luck—will bring love, marriage, and enduring happiness.

Having a Horse in the south of the living room, or the south of the bedroom, often brings the luck of fame and good name to the occupant. A monkey sitting on the horse signifies promotion and upward mobility luck.

Birth years of the Rooster, the Snake, and the Ox

Rooster	Snake	Ox
1933	1933	1925
1945	1941	1937
1957	1953	1949
1969	1965	1961
1981	1977	1973
1993	1989	1985
2005	2001	1997

To find out if the Horse is your peach-blossom animal, refer to the table above. There is more about peach-blossom animals in Tip 182.

The life force of symbols—mystical and ordinary

193

Every spiritual and esoteric tradition has special symbols that seem to carry an intrinsic force for good. The Chinese believe that one can change the quality and movement of energy in any space simply by invoking the power of symbols. These symbols can be as simple as circles and squares, as ordinary as specially potent numbers, and as direct as special characters or words that symbolize something auspicious. They can also be celestial creatures that reflect the chi of other realms of the living world. Totems, divinities, gemstones, and mystical signs are also symbols whose power may be invoked.

The Chinese regard symbols as expressions of the five elements, which have either a yin or a yang manifestation. The concept of yin and yang also has its own symbol—the tai chi symbol. This symbol is a circle made up of a dark half and a light half. It signifies completeness. So when you draw a circle with your hands, you can be invoking the power of the tai chi

Symbols of Fortune
The Pa Kua symbol and symbolic calligraphy (left); the simple symbolism of geometric shapes; and the yin yang, or tai chi, symbol.

Yin yang (tai chi) symbol

symbol. When you fill it with a dark and a light side, you are accessing the two sides of wholeness—both the yin and the yang.

Symbols and the mind
Symbols focus and magnify thoughts. They also transmit messages of intentions and affirmations into the cosmic universal source. Some say this source is the sum of all worlds' consciousnesses, so that, in essence, it represents universal consciousness. This universal source of energy has the power to actualize all states of mind-awareness, knowing, and materializing. When invoked by a knowing mind, symbols take on a powerful resonance that instantly transcends the energy of the space we occupy. The key that unlocks the power of mystical symbols is the mind.

Amulets and Opportunities

I discovered the power of mystical symbols by chance, early in my corporate days, and since then my knowledge of symbols has expanded without me being consciously aware of it. Strangely, symbols seem to appear in my life first, usually as amulets I am asked to wear or carry "for my protection." Over the years, I have become increasingly conscious of

"lucky breaks" related to the timing of benchmark opportunities that have come into my life at certain points, and of last-minute changes of schedule that brought new options to me. All the milestones of my life have been accompanied by symbolic amulets, gemstones, or talismans coming into my possession or into my home just prior to the event.

194 Symbols for power and protection

Symbols may be used to enhance living and working spaces, empower rooms, protect the mind, and expand consciousness with energy tapped directly from the universal divine source. The strategic placement of symbols and the deliberate wearing of them on your body will open the channel to this source of spiritual energy. Symbols are catalysts for revitalizing us in a way that transcends the merely material, although they are themselves often material. They can be made of different substances—metal, wood, or things taken from the earth.

When made of metal, symbols contain powerful energies present in the planetary system. They can be made of gold, silver, copper, brass, aluminum, steel, or combinations of these metals. Metals invoke the power of the Sun, the Moon, Jupiter, Venus, Mercury, Saturn, and Mars. These seven planets symbolize a range of aspirations, attributes, and strengths. Symbols made of metal are said to embody various kinds of good fortune, and different manifestations of courage.

This gold and silver jewelry displays the knot and buckle symbols.

Symbolic Jewelry

Symbols fashioned into jewelry are best made in gold—either yellow or white. When combined with diamonds, they are potentially the most powerful of symbols, because diamonds are the hardest of the earth symbols—the natural crystals of our world that have the exciting potential to unlock and manifest an enormous range of good fortune to those within its sphere of influence. Perhaps this is why the wearing of jewelry fashioned into auspicious symbols is something that has survived since prehistoric times. It is indeed very significant that all the Royal families and cosmic deities of almost every tradition of the world are described as being adorned with gemstones from head to toe.

Consecrating symbols

Symbols need not always be worn to be effective. Wherever they are, they create their own auras, which can usually be strengthened through spiritual consecrations. When symbols come alive through having been consecrated, they emit strong power indeed. Consecration rituals can be as simple as passing symbols over fragrant incense while mantras are chanted (in essence, secret sounds known to spiritual masters), or they can be complicated offering rituals done by holy men who happen to be around.

Totems

Symbols made of wood tend to be favored by more primitive societies. Symbols are often elaborately carved and hung at door entrances and inside houses, and are said to bring long life, blessings from deities, and a natural death. Totems are very popular among many hill peoples in Asia and Native American tribes. Rites of consecration are usually performed for totems, such as the ritualized dotting of the eyes of celestial dragons, or the symbolic taking off in flight of the phoenix that rises from the ashes.

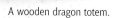

A wooden dragon totem.

Yantra symbols are powerful protectors 195

Hindus invoke the powerful symbols they call yantras for protection and various kinds of specific "good fortune luck." Yantras comprise several triangles, one on top of the other, and these are usually cast as images on large gold coins. The gold usually has the utmost purity. When you visit India, it is a good idea to look for these yantra coins, which usually come as jewelry featuring one of the Indian goddesses of wealth, knowledge, wisdom, or love. Merely having such a yantra medallion in the home creates an auric field around it so that it is protected from negative energies, it is said. There are also planetary yantras, which signify special protections for different days of the week.

The Louvre Pyramid, Paris, France, has strong yin energy that is appropriate for a museum.

Many spiritual traditions regard the triangle as a powerful symbol because it represents the trinity of heaven, earth, and mankind. The triangle also represents the pyramid, which is itself a powerful symbol of preservation. The pyramid is a three-dimensional version of the triangle or Holy Trinity, which can symbolize the family unit as well as the time dimensions of past, present, and future.

A triangle ritual

A powerful Taoist amulet ritual utilizes the triangle symbol. Taoists believe that, when you bury three small crystals (crystal balls or natural single-pointed crystals) in the garden or driveway in front of your main door, positioning them in the form of a triangle with the point facing outward, it is the best possible protection for your house. The energy they create taps into the ground's energy so that it is self-rejuvenating and self-replenishing.

When to avoid the pyramind

Do not place the pyramid symbol inside your home, or on your desk or, worse, live or work in a building that has a pyramid roof line. Pyramids tend to attract and store yin chi and are excellent in the design of yin dwellings, such as tombs. The Louvre Pyramid, in Paris is fine because it is a museum, and its glass structure also feeds light into the corridors that lead to its heart. In the home, however, the pyramid is too powerful a yin symbol. Even for offices and large shopping complexes, the pyramid can be a dangerous symbol and is best avoided.

Yantra designs evoke powerful trinities that underpin many spiritual traditions, such as heaven, earth, and mankind.

196   The symbol of the Lo Shu square—the sigil

Another powerful symbol that is highly respected by masters of the esoteric arts is that of the Lo Shu numbers. It also appears in other traditions. In Indian Vedic astrology, the symbol is referred to as the sigil. A range of forms of planetary numerology about lucky numbers is derived from the sigil that is both intriguing and complex.

A simpler way of tapping into mystical codes is to activate the sign of the sigil. Trace the nine numbers in an ascending order around the nine-grid square illustrated here, and you will derive the sign of the sigil. (Look at the illustration below, which shows how the sigil is formed.) The sign of the sigil is known as the Nine Emperor Sign in Chinese folklore. Using and invoking the sign of the sigil is supposedly one of the secrets of Taoist feng shui; it is said to be the sign to invoke if you want to overcome the negative influence of bad luck numbers flying into your home or office space.

The sigil ritual

Stand outside your home and draw the sign of the sigil as indicated in the illustration. You will see that the numbers are placed where they are according to the Lo Shu square shown here.

Use the hand mudra for invoking mystic symbols (the index and middle fingers point horizontally outwards with the thumb holding down the other two fingers) to draw the sign of the sigil. First, settle your mind, then mentally state your motivation before drawing the sign of the sigil about one foot (30 cm) in front of you, three times. Then quickly draw the zigzag sign before you in order to complete the ritual.

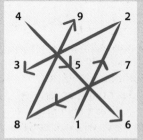

Use the hand mudra for evoking mystic symbols.

This ritual of invoking the sigil at a house entrance is said to release the flow of good chi into a house, thereby overcoming any bad luck, illness, or potential loss.

The Lo Shu and Sigil

1. The Lo Shu Square is one of the most important anchor symbols in the practice of "compass formula feng shui." It is called the Lo Shu square because it is said to have been brought to the legendary Emperor Fu Hsi on the back of a tortoise who floated up along the River Lo in China. The arrangement of the numbers 1 to 9 in the nine-grid square is said to be mystically powerful, and any three of the numbers equal a sum of 15, whether added vertically, horizontally, or diagonally. The number 15 is significant, because this is the number of days it takes a waxing moon to become a full moon, and a waning moon to become a new moon. So the Lo Shu square symbolizes the influence of time on the affairs of mankind.

4	9	2
3	5	7
8	1	6

2. The sigil and the order in which it is drawn is shown here.

Attracting good energy with the sun symbol 197

Another way to benefit your home is to invoke the sun with this powerful symbol that combines the sun's rays with the eight directions of the compass. This mystical symbol features in many advanced ancient systems that utilize a visualized light source for healing work.

Study the symbol carefully. Note the sequence in which it is drawn and the direction of the strokes. Use your fingers to draw this symbol in the rooms of your home that need a dose of sun energy. As you draw it, imagine that you are creating a ball of brilliant light then visualize the sun's brilliant rays emanating outward from it and washing your rooms with powerful light energy.This is a very potent mystical symbol that requires a simple visualization. It sends light rays into your living space. Do remember to complete the ritual with the zigzag hand movement.

When to use the sun symbol

A good time to use this is when someone in your house is ill, or having a long period of bad luck in terms of opportunities drying up or losing a job. It strengthens and revitalizes the energy present, and improves things for those who are suffering. For someone who is very ill, imagine tapping into the light source of the sun and bringing the light into the room occupied by the sick person. This symbol has the power to create additional energy that will help anyone feel better.

As you invoke mystical symbols to call upon the universal source of energy, it is really helpful to generate the motivation of selfless compassion within yourself. Think positive thoughts as you perform this ritual. Mystical symbols always work best when your thoughts and intentions are good. The more unconditional and altruistic the energy of love that is used to empower the invoking of a particular symbol, then the more powerful it will be.

The sun symbol can be used for powerful healing and energizing. Draw it in the air, following the sequence illustrated below. It can also be displayed in art, or here, as part of a mirror design, to attract positive yang energy into a room.

2

3

4

198 Creating personal symbols

There are many different symbols we can invoke to improve the sense of sanctuary and comfort of a living space. Keeping homes clean and filled with vitality through the different realms of our consciousness often require us to raise our awareness of the different realms of chi in our environment. Only then can we enjoy the good things of the material world and also find inner happiness that transcends time and space.

In the world of mind, body, and spirit, we can choose a host of transcendental allies who may become our personal bodyguards and protectors. These might be from the animal or bird world. We also can choose symbols from deep within the earth—stones of every shape, size or color—or objects from the ocean depths: pearls, seashells, seaweeds, or exotic fish. The creation of personal symbols is not unlike the making of personal amulets and talismans.

Symbols that are public rather than personal become business insignias or brands that express a company's values.

How Crystals Became Me

When you practice focusing your consciousness to empower objects and symbols, they gain strength simply because you imbue them with strength. I first suspected this to be so when I was in my twenties. I had always had an affinity with natural crystals, so in the Seventies when I first became aware that I could not resist the few single-pointed crystals that came my way, I went along with my instincts and indulged myself with them. From then on, crystals just kept coming to me. People would make me the most stunning gifts of single and double-pointed crystals, and I would find crystal clusters being mailed to me all the time.

I always cleansed and empowered them. For this, I used fragrance and incense and, when I chanted mantras and did my meditations, they would always be nearby.

My collection has since expanded into crystal balls purchased from all over the world and crystal malas (i.e., beads strung into Buddhist rosaries comprising 108 beads). And, of course, I am also a great believer in wearing colored precious stones set with gold and diamonds. Every piece of crystal I own today brings me wonderful feelings of security and well-being. I feel revitalized each time I stroke and hold my crystals.

In short, they have become my personal symbols.

Index

Picture Credits